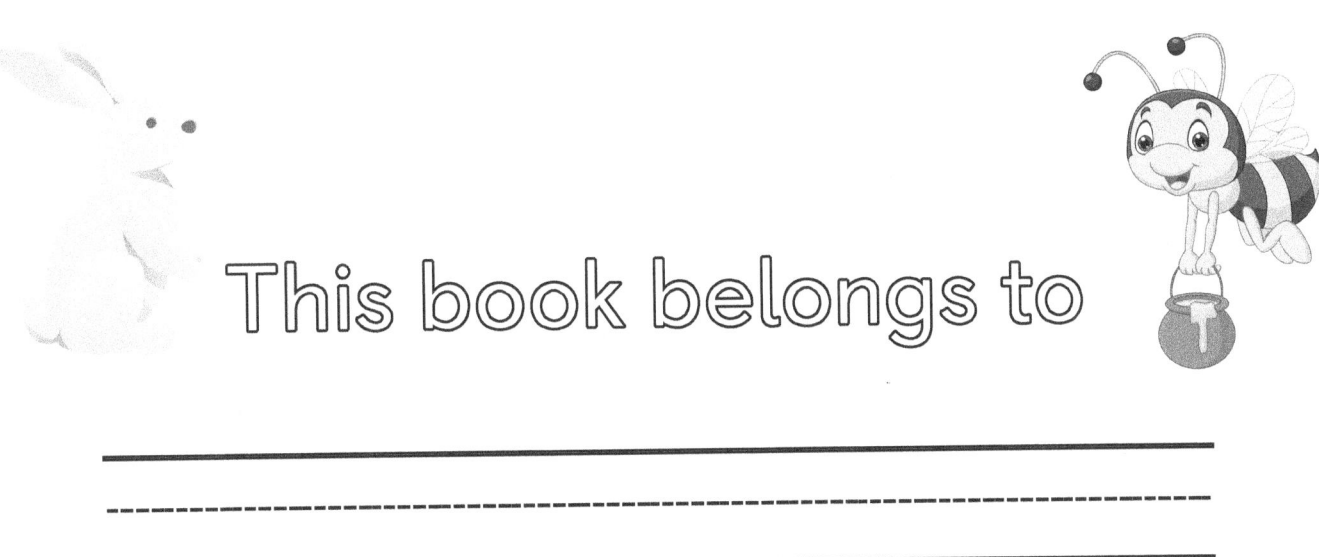

This book belongs to

_____

Grade: _____

School: _____

Sight words, also known as high-frequency words, are words that frequently occur in both reading and writing. "Fry's 1st 100 Sight Words Practice Book for Kindergarten and Grade 1 Kids" is a beginner's level practice book that contains the first 100 high-frequency words for children to learn and write.

This practice book is thoughtfully sequenced to help build children's learning and writing abilities through fun coloring activities. The book provides children with the opportunity to practice spelling and sight words, encouraging engagement throughout by integrating tracing, writing, and coloring activities. The fundamentals of the book, including dot-to-dot tracing, improve children's handwriting, and foster a motivation to write independently.

The book commences with the practice of basic strokes, advancing to learning sight words through tracing and writing, and utilizing sight word flashcards to practice and track learning progress. Furthermore, the book provides uppercase and lowercase letter tracing charts, a summary chart of sight words, and concludes with a completion certificate as a token of appreciation.

This book, suitable for both Kindergarten and Grade 1 students, is an excellent resource for developing the essential skills of reading and writing in children.

Table of Contents:

FRY's 1st 100 SIGHT WORDS

PRACTICE BOOK
For Kindergarten & Grade 1

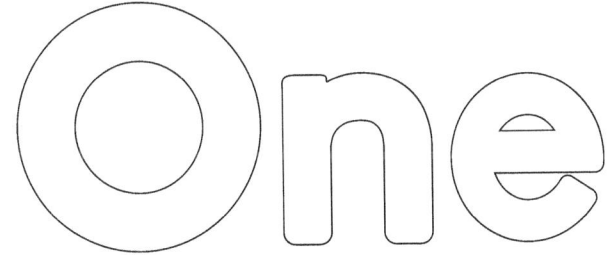

One

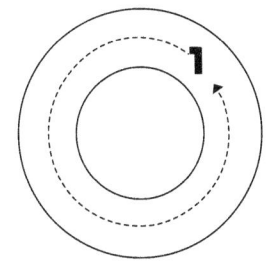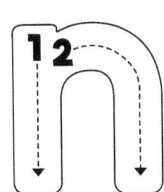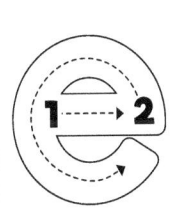

One

COLORING

Ages 4+

TRACING

Greetings, wonderful parents!

Thank you for choosing this amazing book to help your child learn Fry's First 100 Sight Words. We hope you're just as excited as we are to begin this learning journey!

Your feedback is incredibly valuable to us. Please take a moment to leave a review on the platform where you purchased the book, and let us know what you thought. We're always striving to make our resources better and more effective, and your insights will help us do just that.

And, if you're ready for more learning adventures, check out our other books in the series. We promise they're just as fantastic as this one!

Thanks again for your support, and happy learning!

Best regards,

abcZbook Press
www.abczbook.com

abcZbook Press

Basic strokes practice

Basic strokes practice

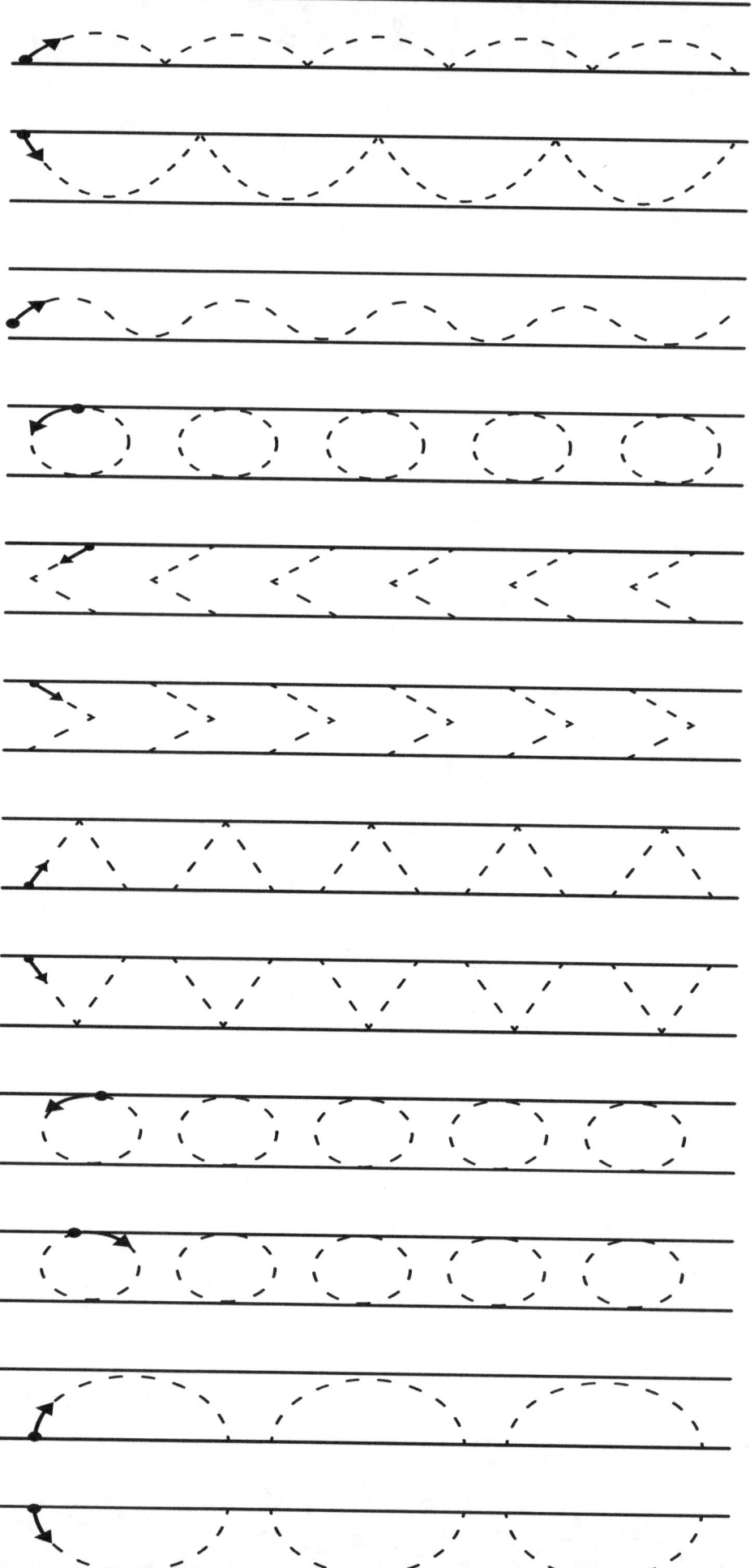

Basic strokes practice

Read the word:

Color the word:

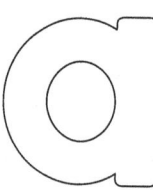

Trace the word:

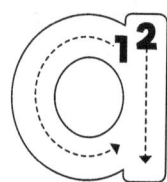

Trace the word:

Write the word:

_____

- -

_____

Read the word:

about

Color the word:

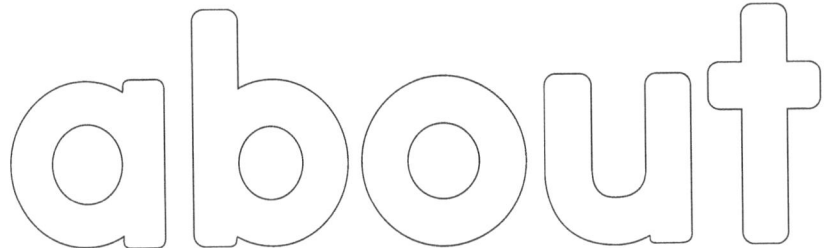

Trace the word:

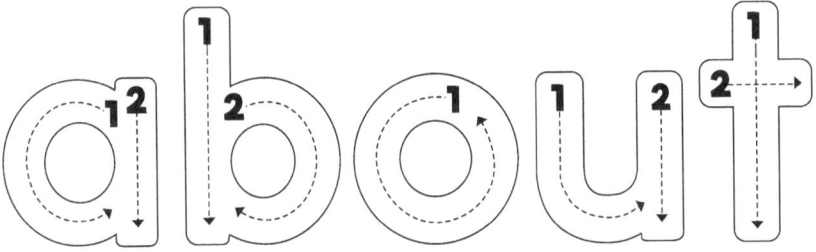

Trace the word:

Write the word:

about

Read the word:

Color the word:

Trace the word:

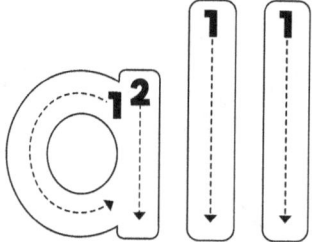

Trace the word:

Write the word:

_____

_____

Read the word:

Color the word:

Trace the word:

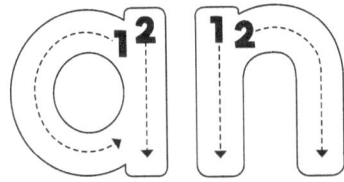

Trace the word:

Write the word:

Read the word:

Color the word:

Trace the word:

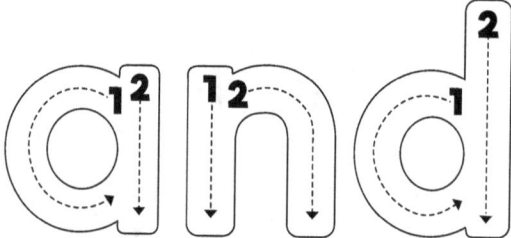

Trace the word:

Write the word:

Read the word:

Color the word:

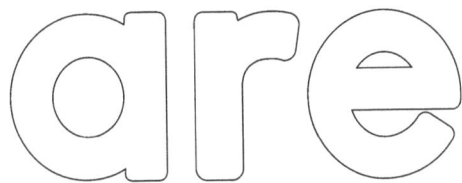

Trace the word:

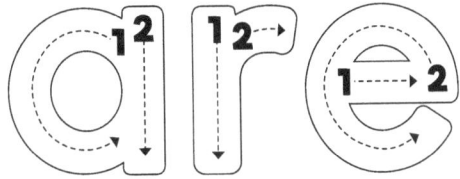

Trace the word:

Write the word:

Read the word:

Color the word:

Trace the word:

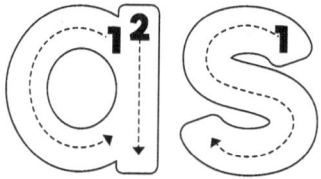

Trace the word:

Write the word:

Read the word:

Color the word:

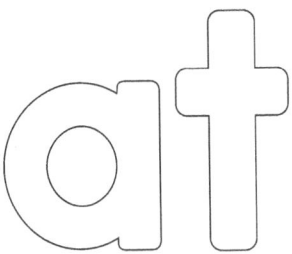

Trace the word:

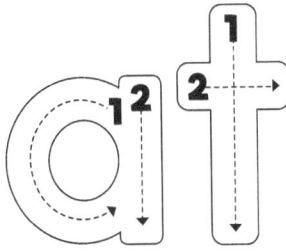

Trace the word:

Write the word:

Read the word:

Color the word:

Trace the word:

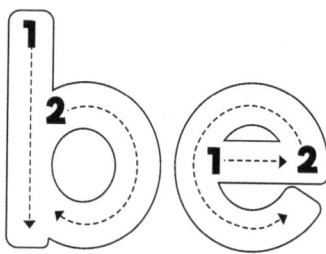

Trace the word:

Write the word:

Read the word:

Color the word:

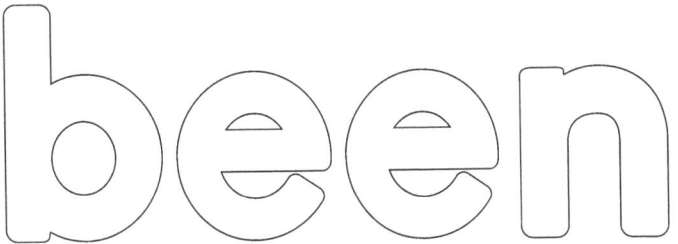

Trace the word:

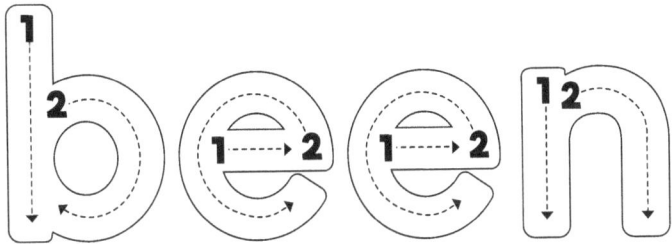

Trace the word:

Write the word:

Read the word:

Color the word:

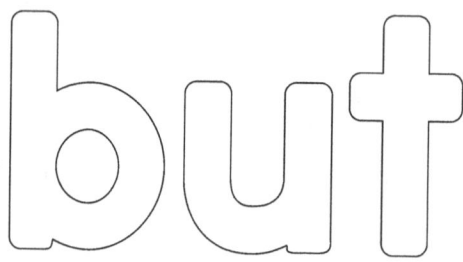

Trace the word:

Trace the word:

Write the word:

Read the word:

Color the word:

Trace the word:

Trace the word:

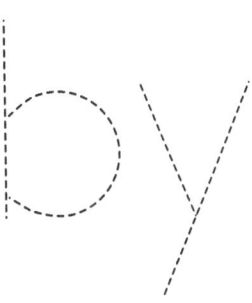

Write the word:

Read the word:

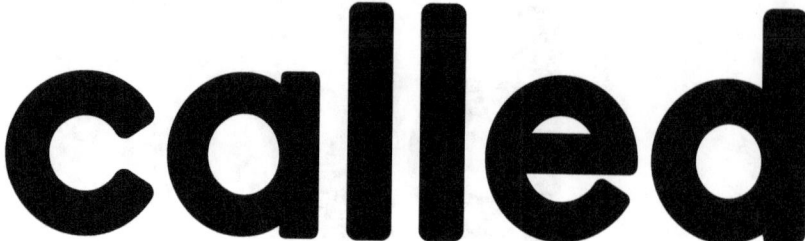

Color the word:

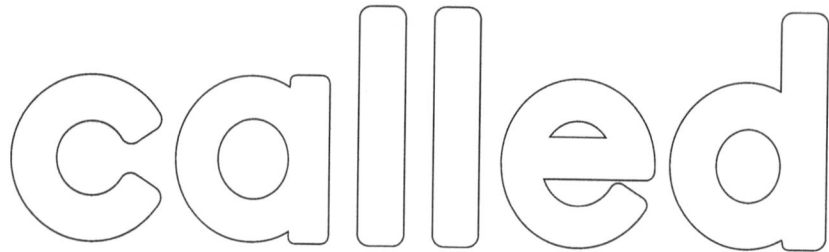

Trace the word:

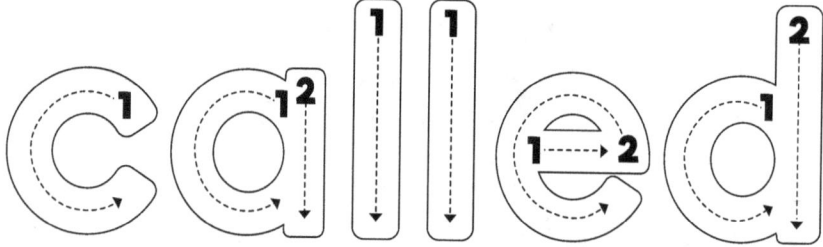

Trace the word:

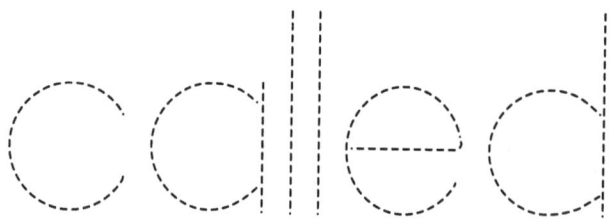

Write the word:

Read the word:

Color the word:

Trace the word:

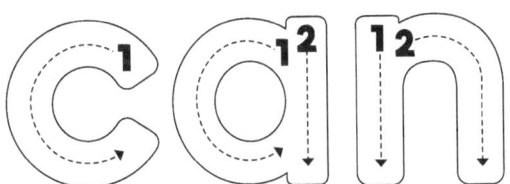

Trace the word:

Write the word:

Read the word:

Color the word:

Trace the word:

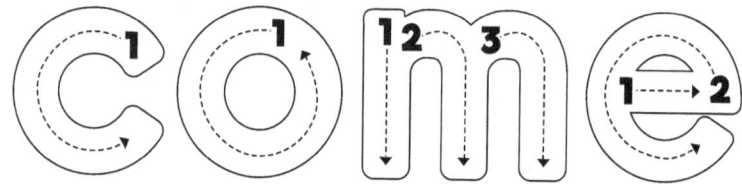

Trace the word:

Write the word:

Read the word:

Color the word:

Trace the word:

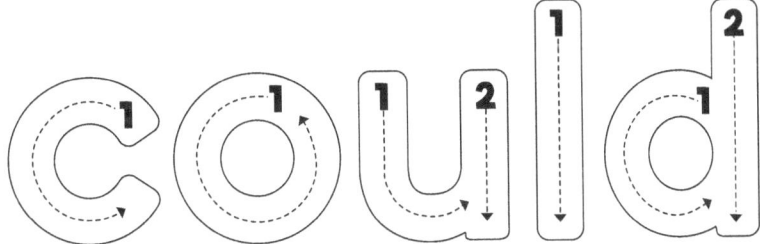

Trace the word:

Write the word:

_____

_____

Read the word:

Color the word:

Trace the word:

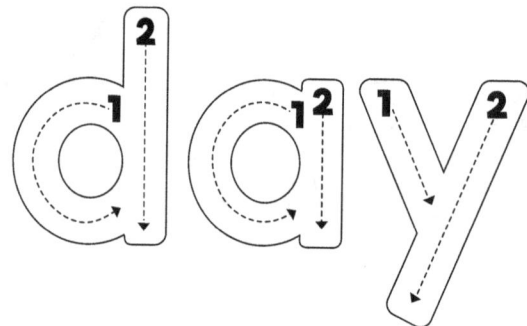

Trace the word:

Write the word:

Read the word:

Color the word:

Trace the word:

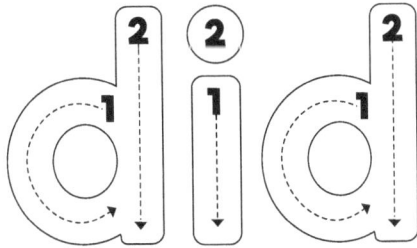

Trace the word:

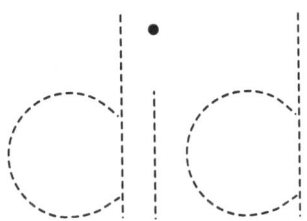

Write the word:

Read the word:

Color the word:

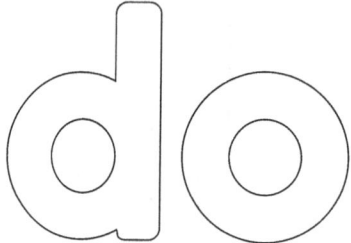

Trace the word:

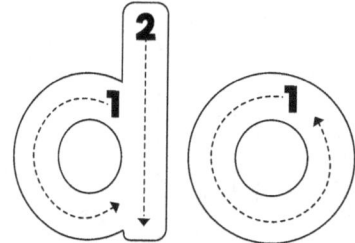

Trace the word:

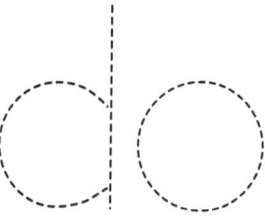

Write the word:

Read the word:

Color the word:

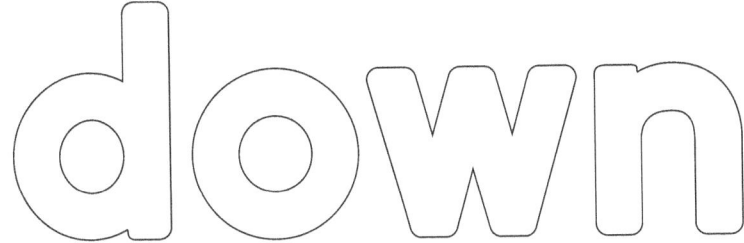

Trace the word:

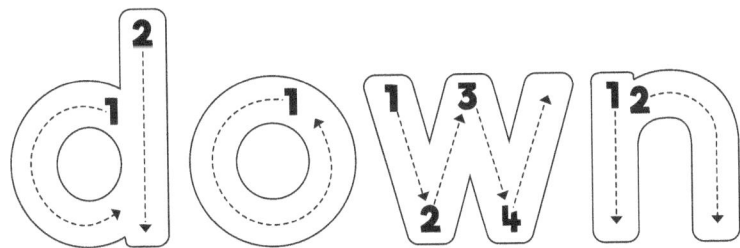

Trace the word:

Write the word:

_____

_____

Read the word:

Color the word:

Trace the word:

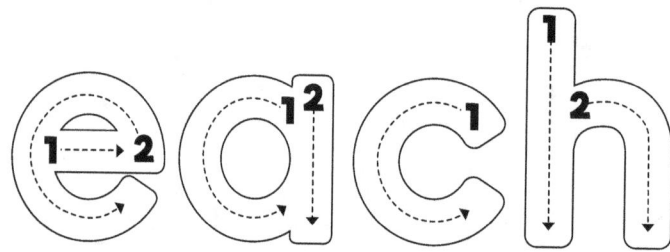

Trace the word:

Write the word:

Read the word:

Color the word:

Trace the word:

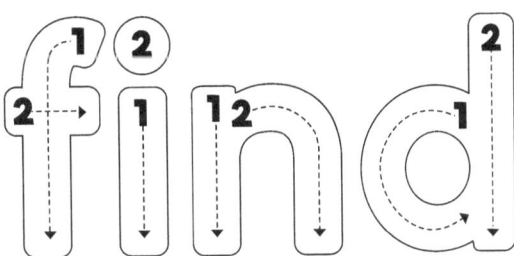

Trace the word:

Write the word:

Read the word:

Color the word:

Trace the word:

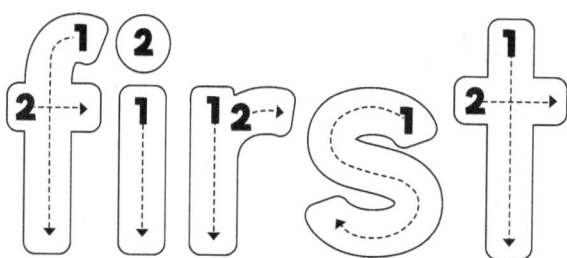

Trace the word:

Write the word:

Read the word:

Color the word:

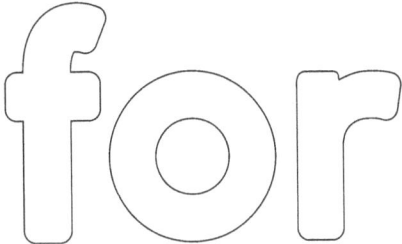

Trace the word:

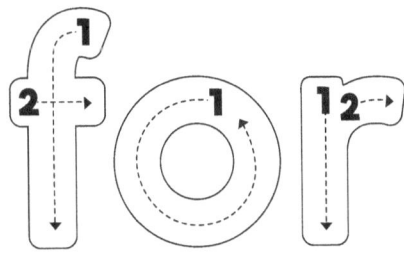

Trace the word:

Write the word:

_____

_____

Read the word:

Color the word:

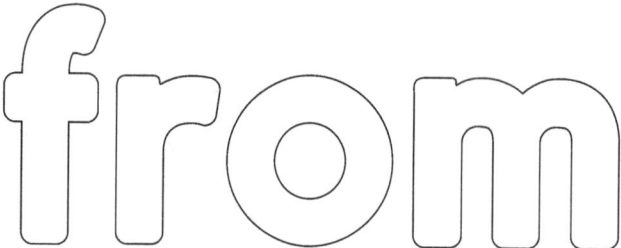

Trace the word:

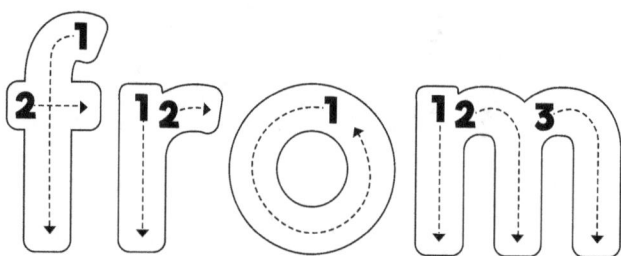

Trace the word:

Write the word:

Read the word:

Color the word:

Trace the word:

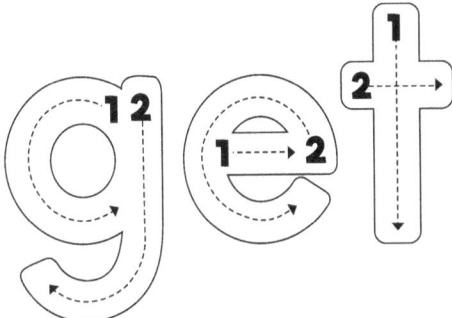

Trace the word:

Write the word:

Read the word:

Color the word:

Trace the word:

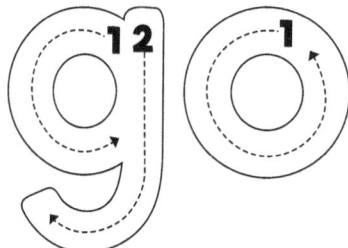

Trace the word:

Write the word:

_____

- -

_____

Read the word:

Color the word:

Trace the word:

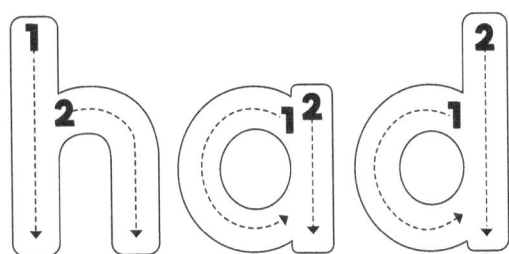

Trace the word:

Write the word:

_____

_____

Read the word:

Color the word:

Trace the word:

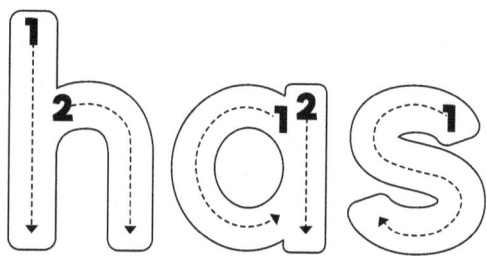

Trace the word:

Write the word:

Read the word:

Color the word:

Trace the word:

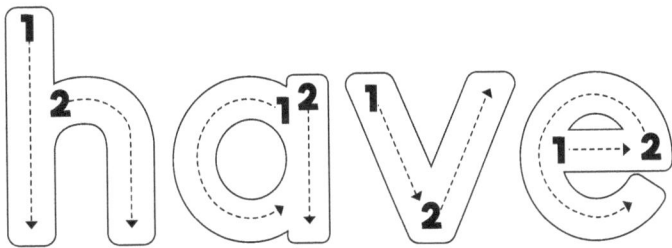

Trace the word:

Write the word: _____

Read the word:

Color the word:

Trace the word:

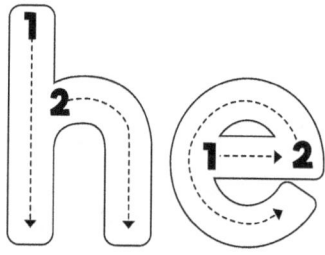

Trace the word:

Write the word:

Read the word:

Color the word:

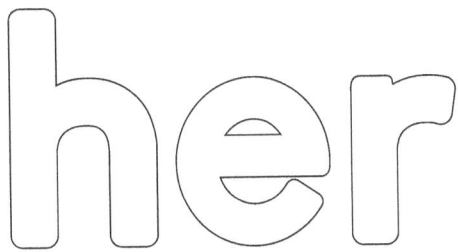

Trace the word:

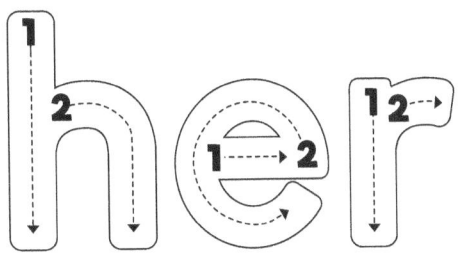

Trace the word:

Write the word:

Read the word:

Color the word:

Trace the word:

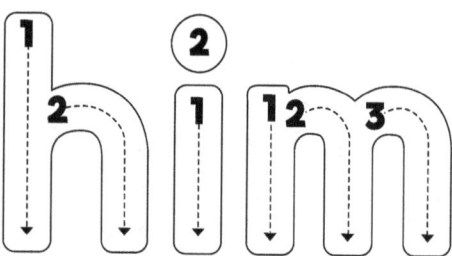

Trace the word:

Write the word:

_____

- -

_____

Read the word:

Color the word:

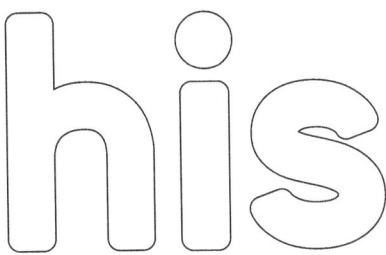

Trace the word:

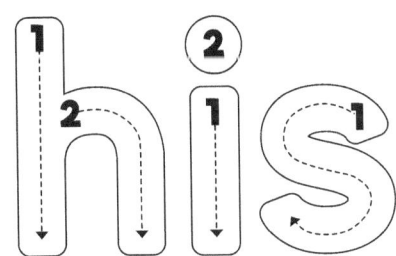

Trace the word:

Write the word:

Read the word:

Color the word:

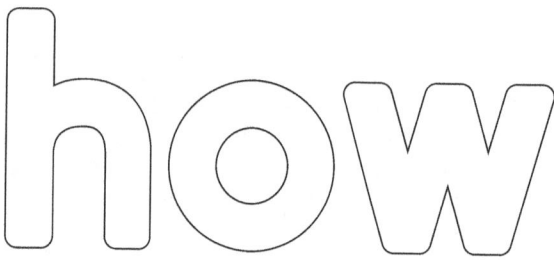

Trace the word:

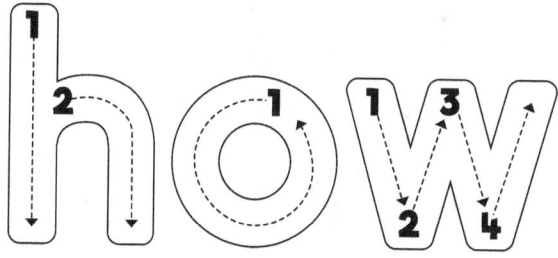

Trace the word:

Write the word:

Read the word:

Color the word:

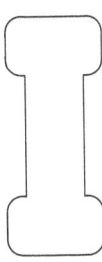

Trace the word:

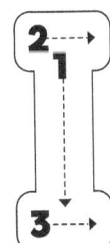

Trace the word:

Write the word:

Read the word:

Color the word:

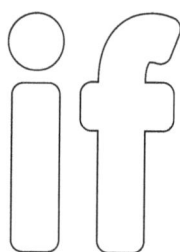

Trace the word:

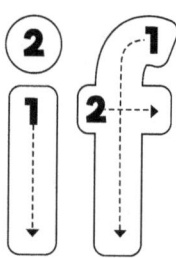

Trace the word:

Write the word:

Read the word:

Color the word:

Trace the word:

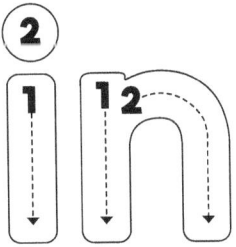

Trace the word:

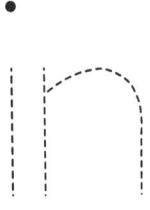

Write the word:

Read the word:

Color the word:

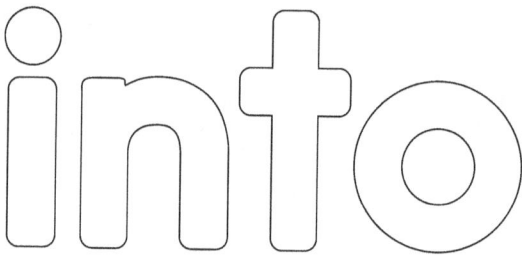

Trace the word:

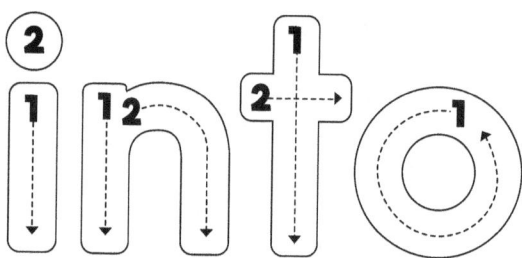

Trace the word:

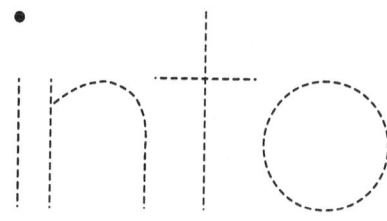

Write the word:

Read the word:

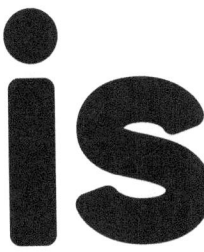

Color the word:

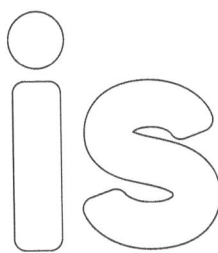

Trace the word:

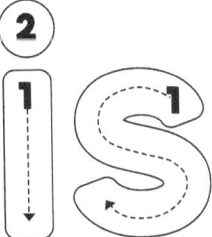

Trace the word:

Write the word:

Read the word:

Color the word:

Trace the word:

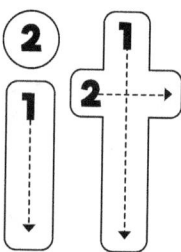

Trace the word:

Write the word:

Read the word:

Color the word:

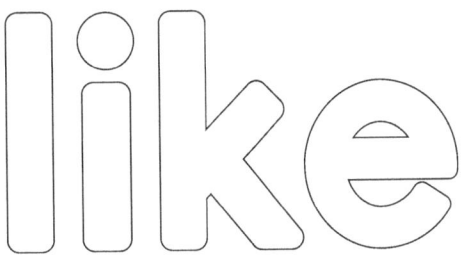

Trace the word:

Trace the word:

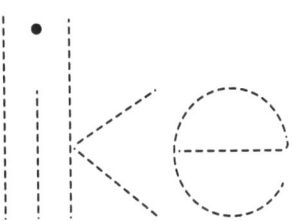

Write the word:

_____

_____

Read the word:

Color the word:

Trace the word:

Trace the word:

Write the word:

Read the word:

Color the word:

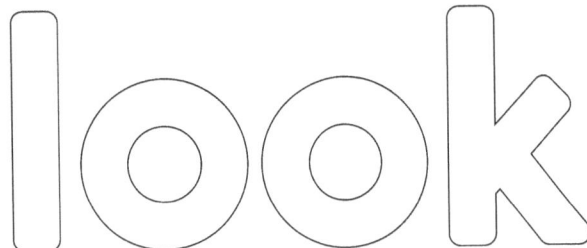

Trace the word:

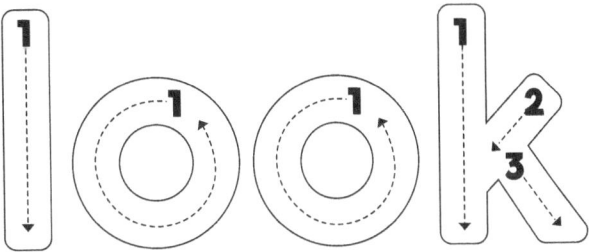

Trace the word:

Write the word:

_____

_____

Read the word:

Color the word:

Trace the word:

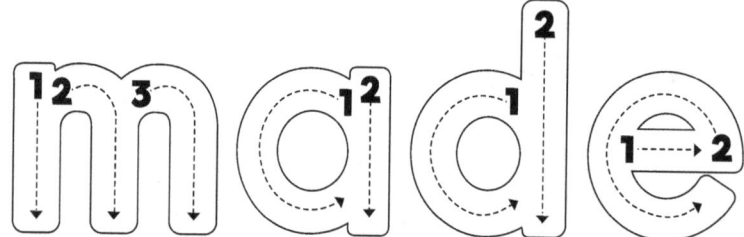

Trace the word:

Write the word:

Read the word:

Color the word:

Trace the word:

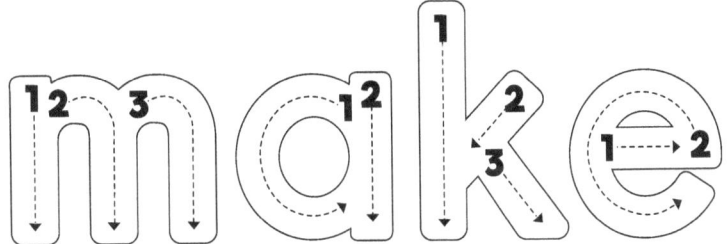

Trace the word:

Write the word:

_____

_____

Read the word:

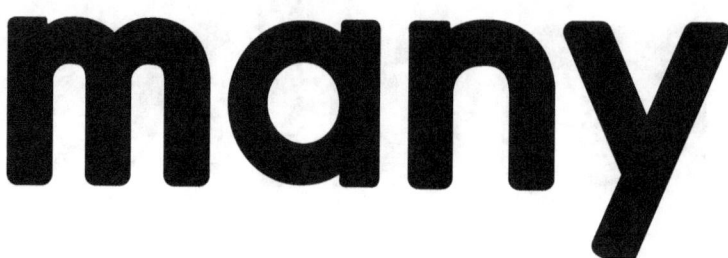

Color the word:

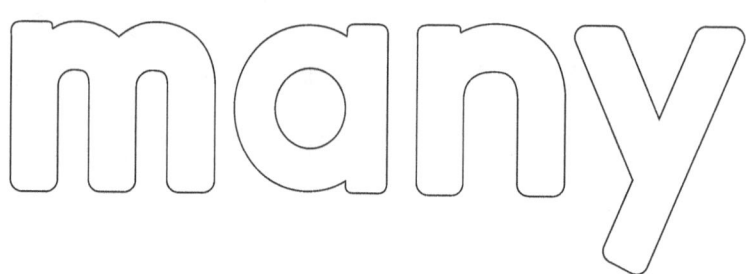

Trace the word:

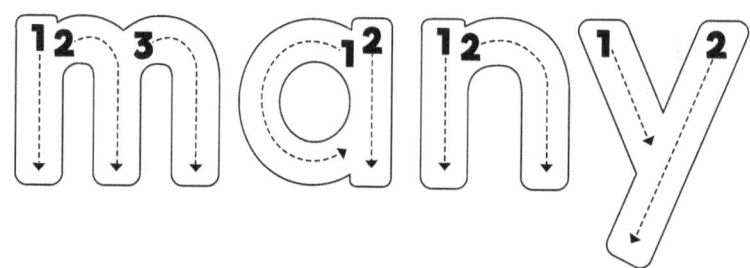

Trace the word:

Write the word:

Read the word:

Color the word:

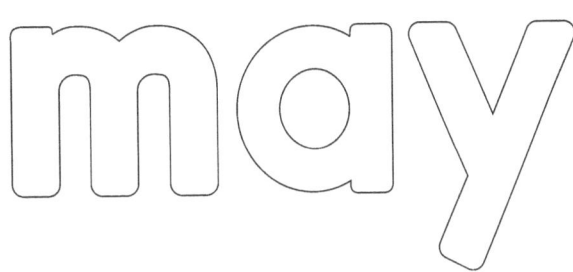

Trace the word:

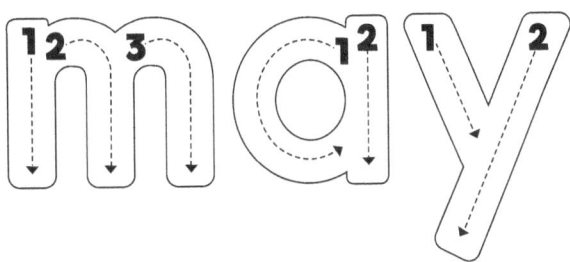

Trace the word:

Write the word:

Read the word:

Color the word:

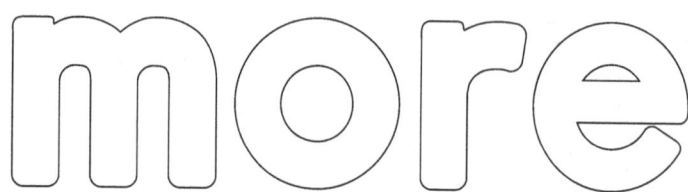

Trace the word:

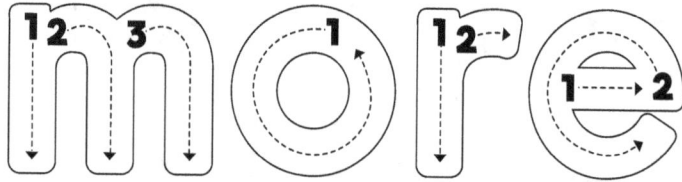

Trace the word:

Write the word:

Read the word:

Color the word:

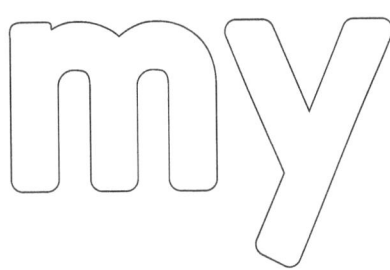

Trace the word:

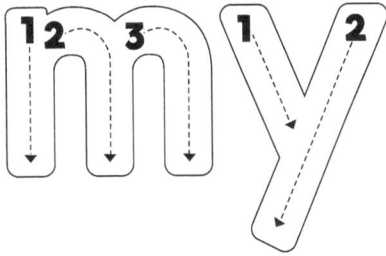

Trace the word:

Write the word:

_____

_____

Read the word:

Color the word:

Trace the word:

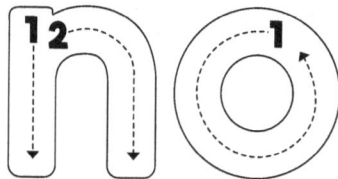

Trace the word:

Write the word:

Read the word:

Color the word:

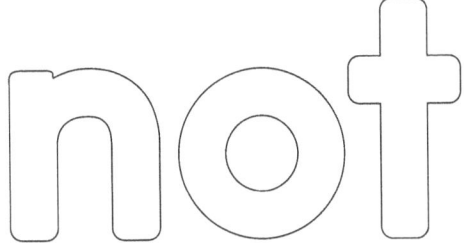

Trace the word:

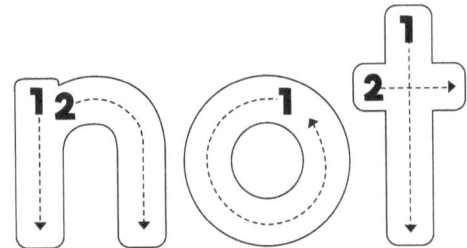

Trace the word:

Write the word:

Read the word:

Color the word:

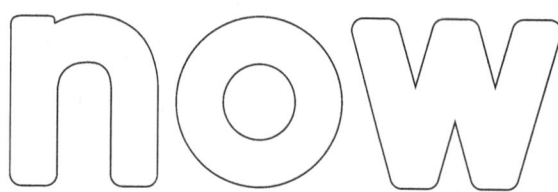

Trace the word:

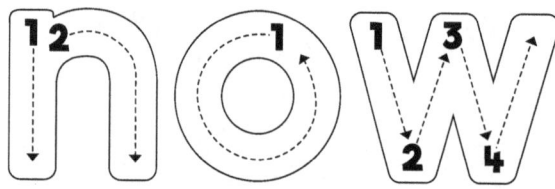

Trace the word:

Write the word:

Read the word:

number

Color the word:

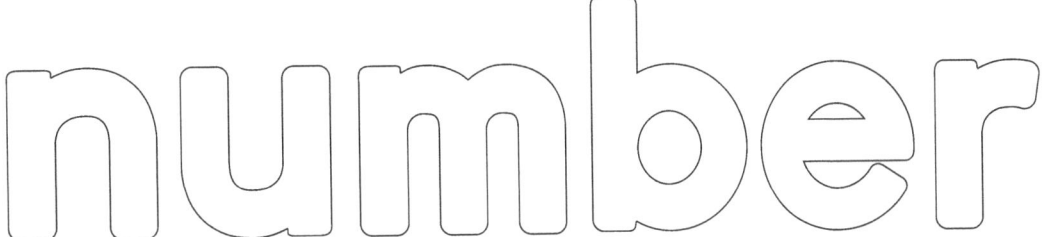

Trace the word:

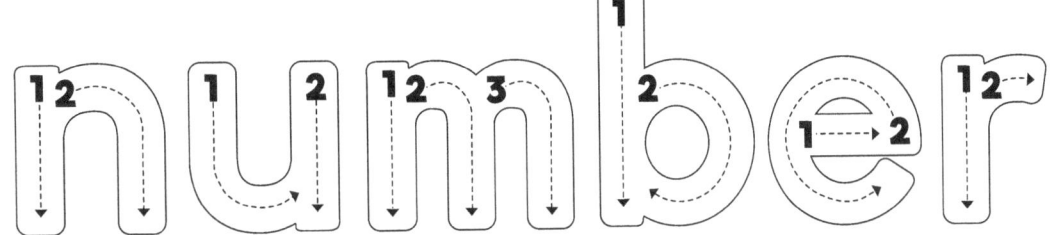

Trace the word:

Write the word:

Read the word:

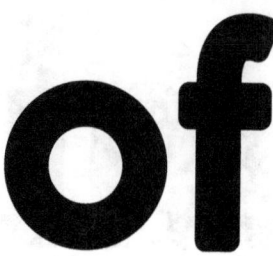

Color the word:

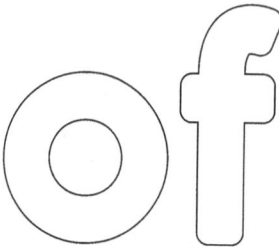

Trace the word:

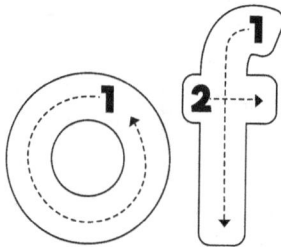

Trace the word:

Write the word:

Read the word:

Color the word:

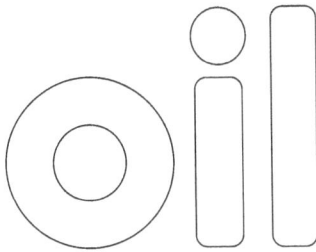

Trace the word:

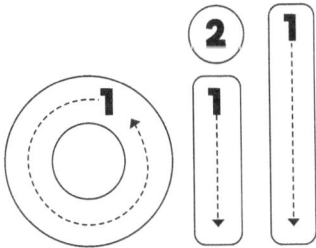

Trace the word:

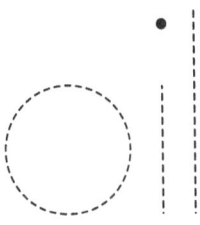

Write the word:

Read the word:

Color the word:

Trace the word:

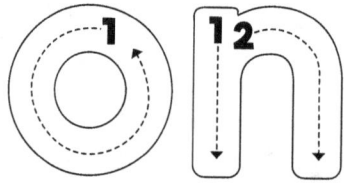

Trace the word:

Write the word:

_____

- -

_____

Read the word:

Color the word:

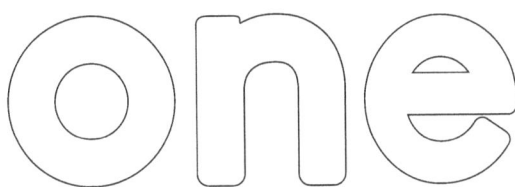

Trace the word:

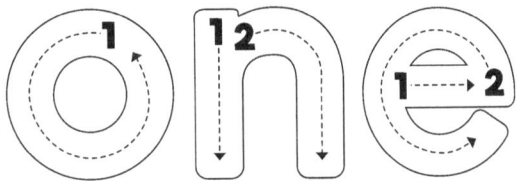

Trace the word:

Write the word:

_____

- -

_____

Read the word:

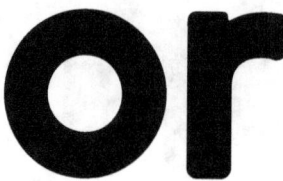

Color the word:

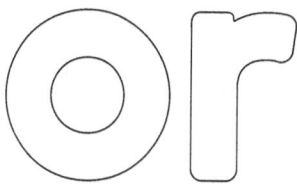

Trace the word:

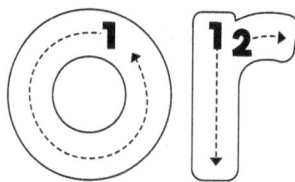

Trace the word:

Write the word:

_____

_____

Read the word:

other

Color the word:

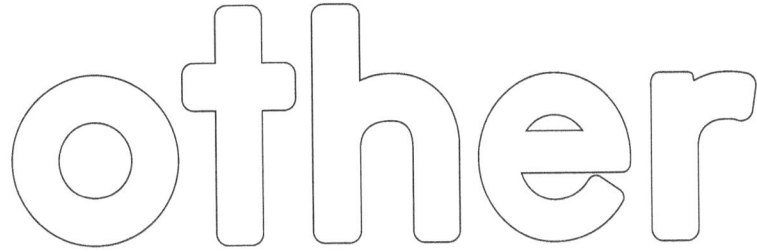

Trace the word:

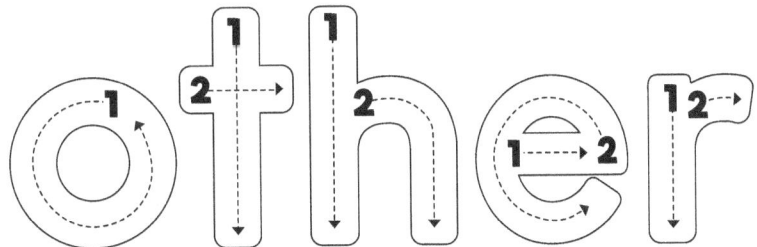

Trace the word:

Write the word:

Read the word:

Color the word:

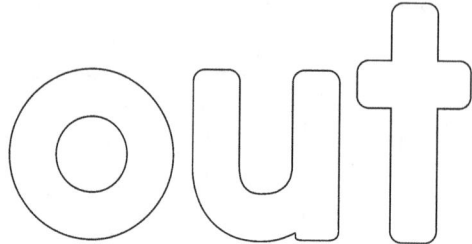

Trace the word:

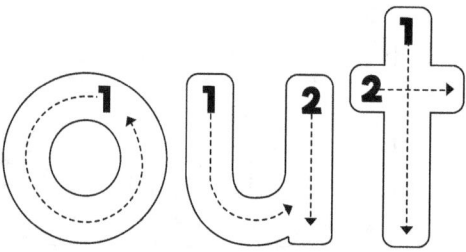

Trace the word:

Write the word:

_____

_____

Read the word:

Color the word:

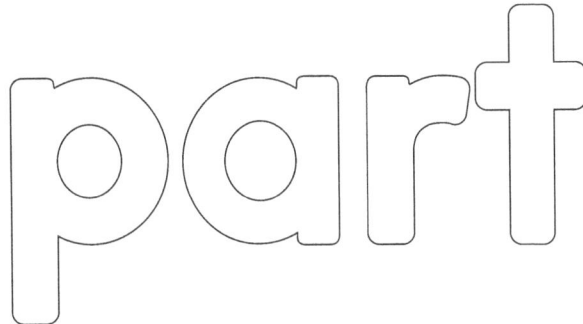

Trace the word:

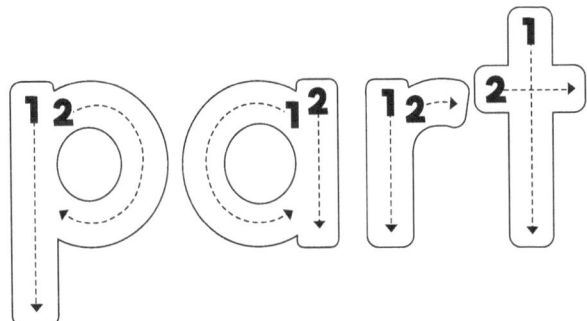

Trace the word:

Write the word:

Read the word:

Color the word:

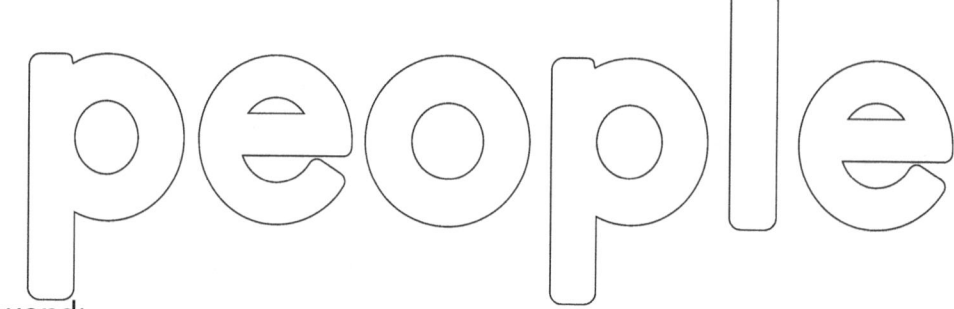

Trace the word:

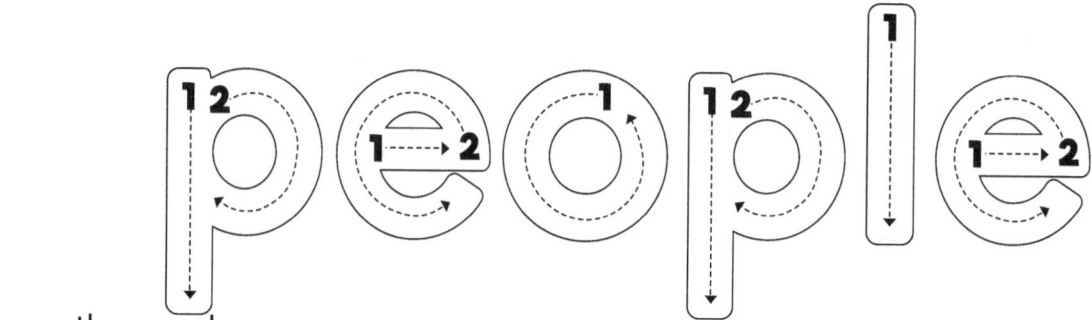

Trace the word:

Write the word:

_____

_____

Read the word:

Color the word:

Trace the word:

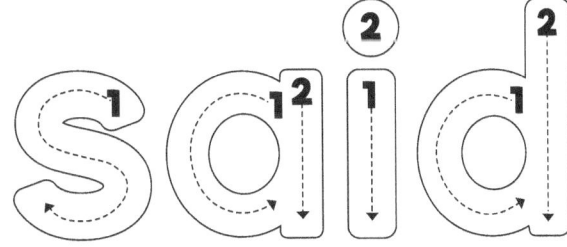

Trace the word:

Write the word:

Read the word:

Color the word:

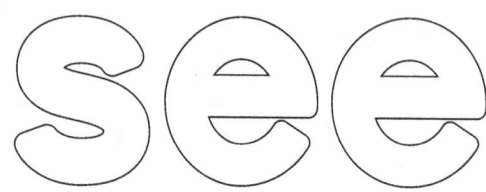

Trace the word:

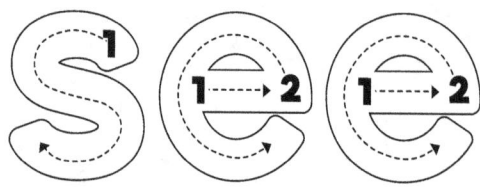

Trace the word:

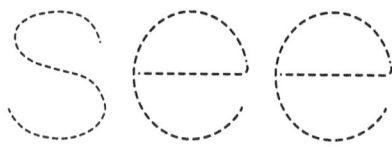

Write the word:

_____

· ·

_____

Read the word:

Color the word:

Trace the word:

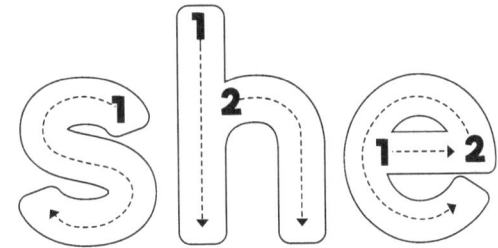

Trace the word:

Write the word:

Read the word:

Color the word:

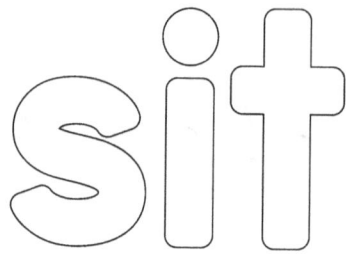

Trace the word:

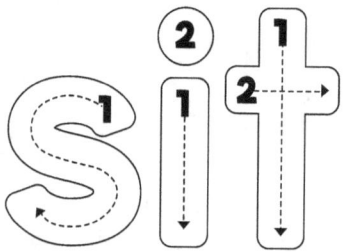

Trace the word:

Write the word:

Read the word:

Color the word:

Trace the word:

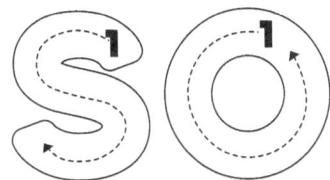

Trace the word:

Write the word:

Read the word:

Color the word:

Trace the word:

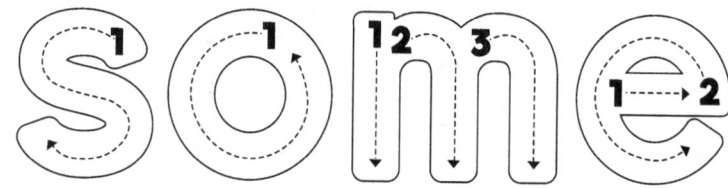

Trace the word:

Write the word:

. . . .

Read the word:

Color the word:

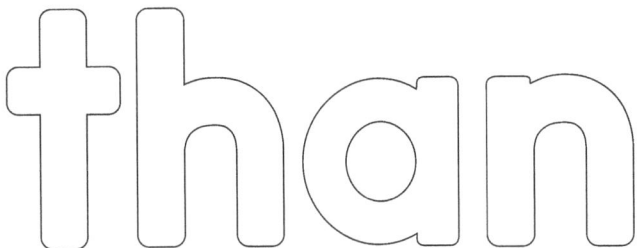

Trace the word:

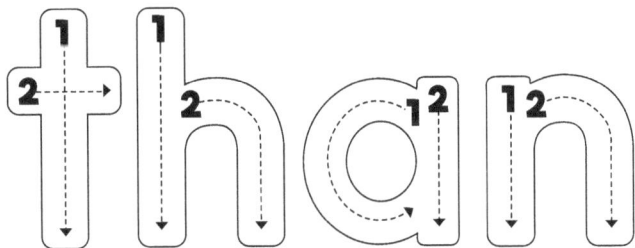

Trace the word:

Write the word:

_____

_____

Read the word:

Color the word:

Trace the word:

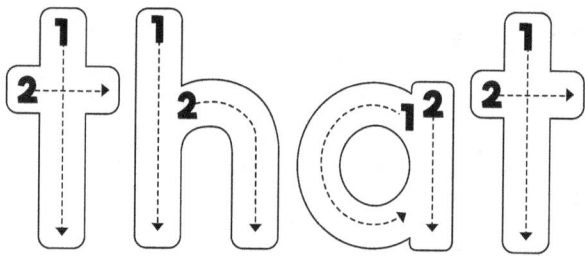

Trace the word:

Write the word:

_____

- -

_____

Read the word:

Color the word:

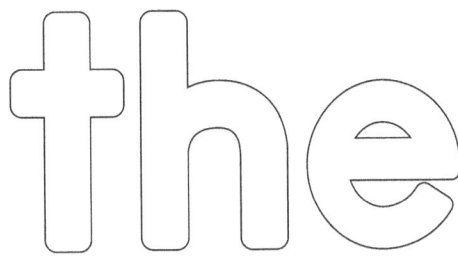

Trace the word:

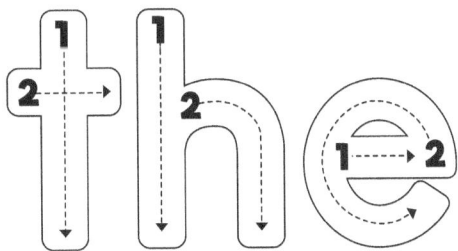

Trace the word:

Write the word:

_____

- -

_____

Read the word:

Color the word:

Trace the word:

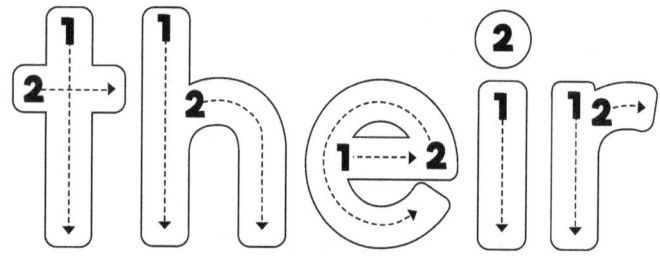

Trace the word:

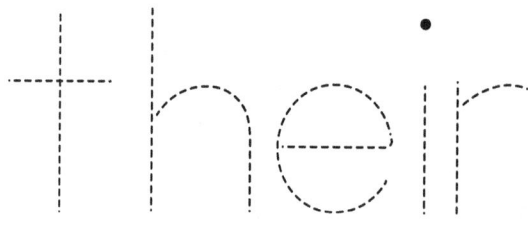

Write the word:

Read the word:

Color the word:

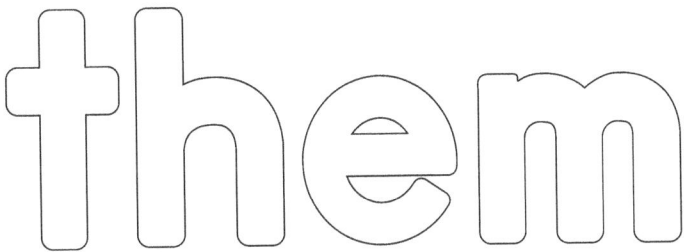

Trace the word:

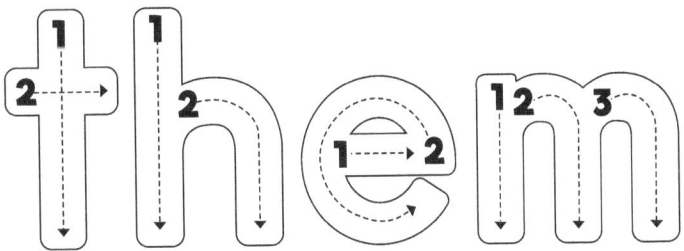

Trace the word:

Write the word:

_____

. . . . them . . . .

_____

Read the word:

Color the word:

Trace the word:

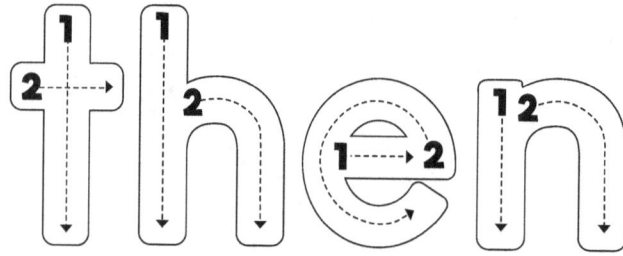

Trace the word:

Write the word:

Read the word:

Color the word:

Trace the word:

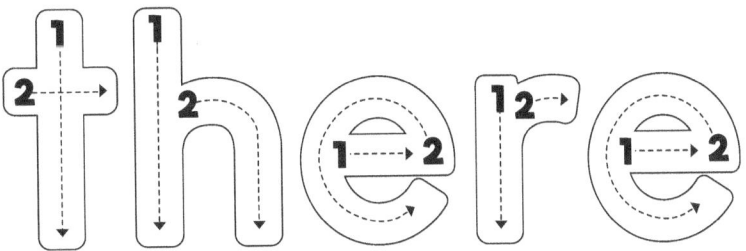

Trace the word:

Write the word:

Read the word:

these

Color the word:

Trace the word:

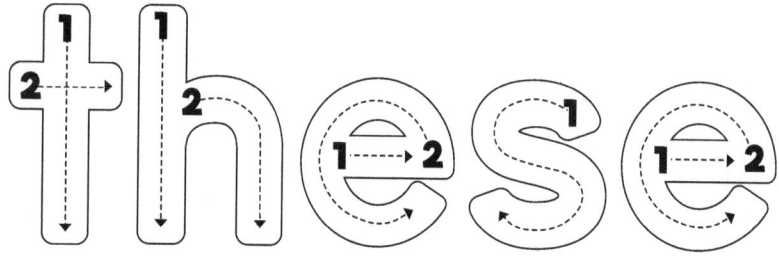

Trace the word:

Write the word:

Read the word:

Color the word:

Trace the word:

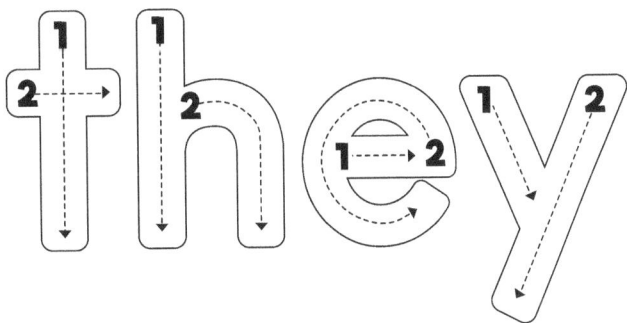

Trace the word:

Write the word:

_____

_____

Read the word:

Color the word:

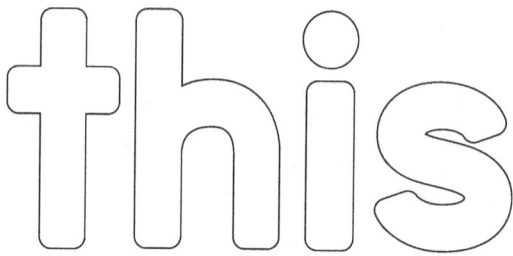

Trace the word:

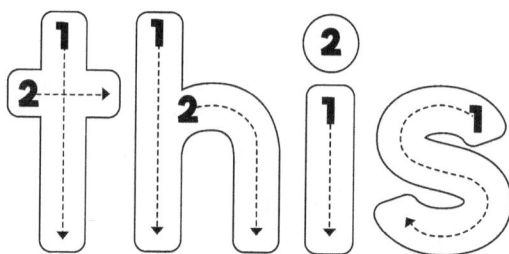

Trace the word:

Write the word:

Read the word:

Color the word:

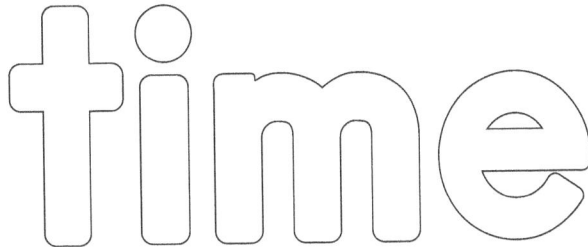

Trace the word:

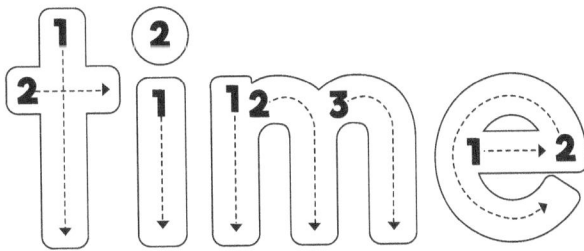

Trace the word:

Write the word:

Read the word:

Color the word:

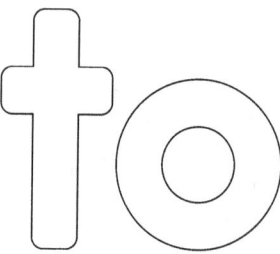

Trace the word:

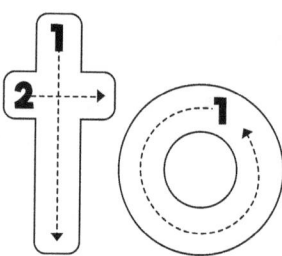

Trace the word:

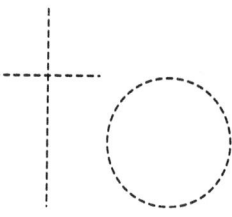

Write the word:

_____

- -

_____

Read the word:

Color the word:

Trace the word:

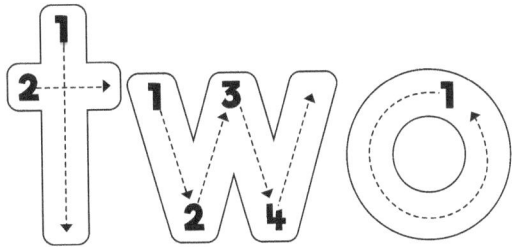

Trace the word:

Write the word:

Read the word:

Color the word:

Trace the word:

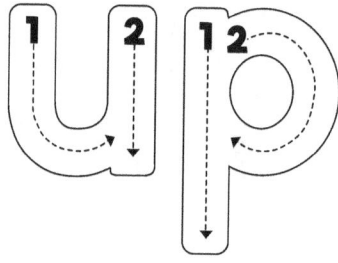

Trace the word:

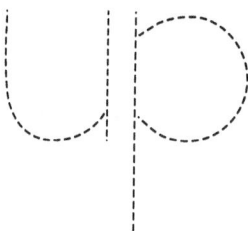

Write the word:

Read the word:

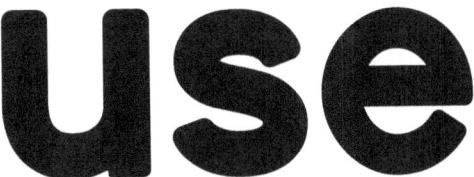

Color the word:

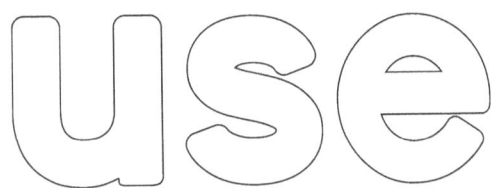

Trace the word:

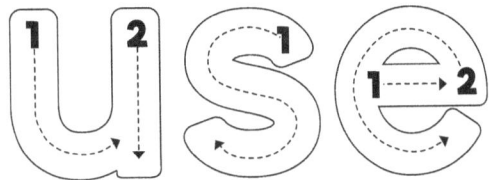

Trace the word:

Write the word:

Read the word:

Color the word:

Trace the word:

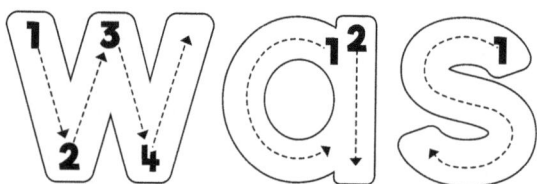

Trace the word:

Write the word:

Read the word:

Color the word:

Trace the word:

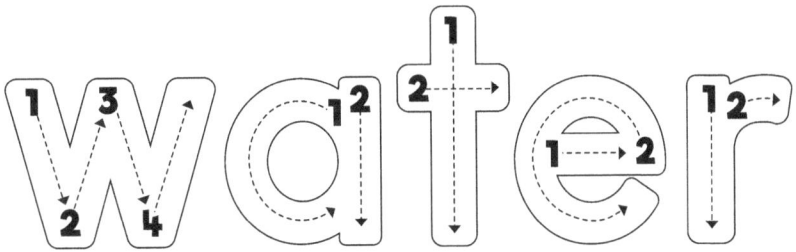

Trace the word:

Write the word: _____

_____

Read the word:

Color the word:

Trace the word:

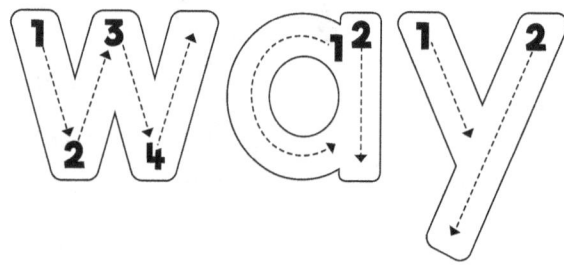

Trace the word:

Write the word:

_____

- -

_____

Read the word:

Color the word:

Trace the word:

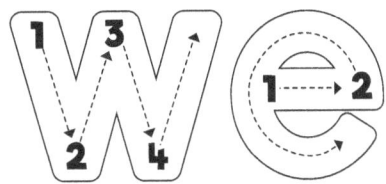

Trace the word:

Write the word:

_____

_____

Read the word:

Color the word:

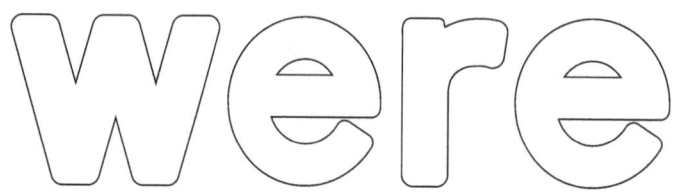

Trace the word:

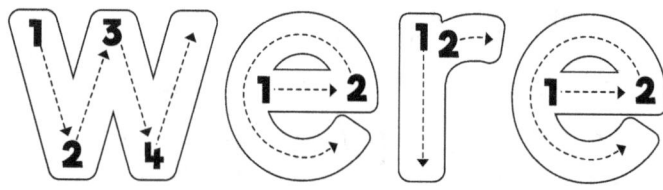

Trace the word:

Write the word:

_____

- -

_____

Read the word:

Color the word:

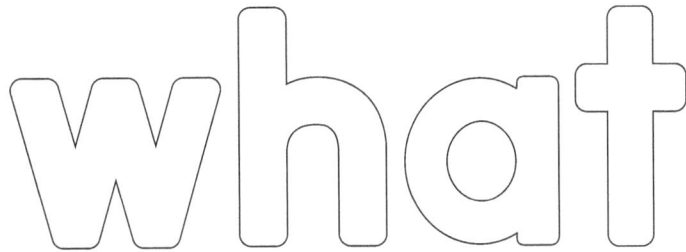

Trace the word:

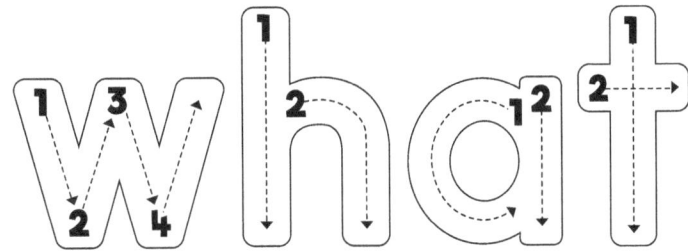

Trace the word:

Write the word:

_____

- -

_____

Read the word:

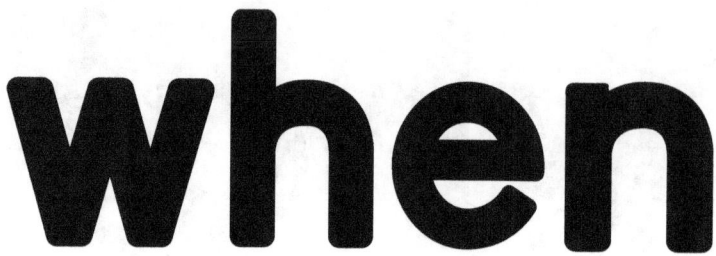

Color the word:

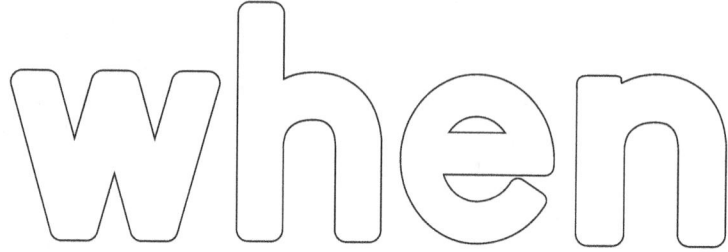

Trace the word:

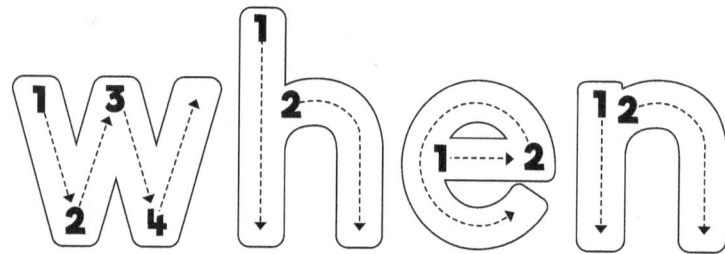

Trace the word:

Write the word:

Read the word:

Color the word:

Trace the word:

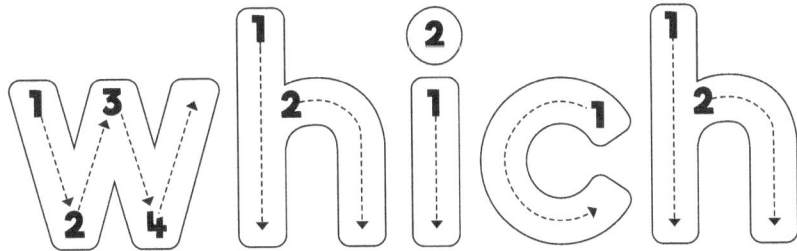

Trace the word:

Write the word:

Read the word:

Color the word:

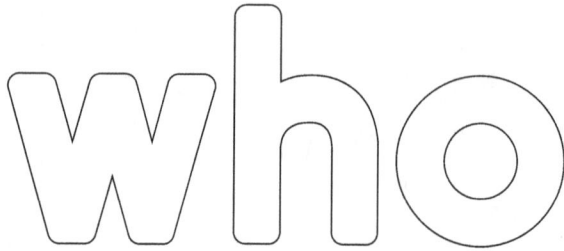

Trace the word:

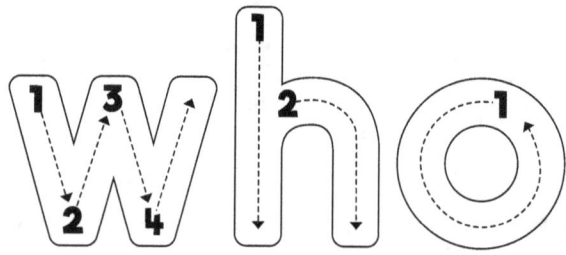

Trace the word:

Write the word:

Read the word:

Color the word:

Trace the word:

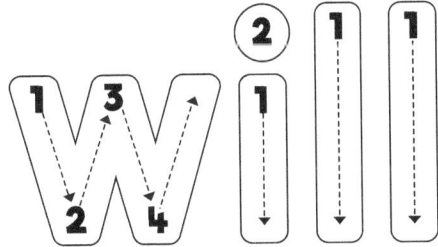

Trace the word:

Write the word:

Read the word:

Color the word:

Trace the word:

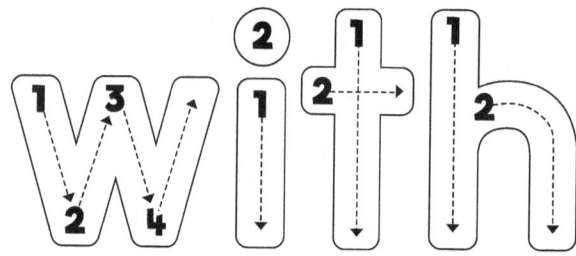

Trace the word:

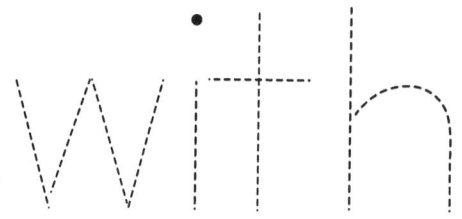

Write the word:

_____

....

_____

Read the word:

Color the word:

Trace the word:

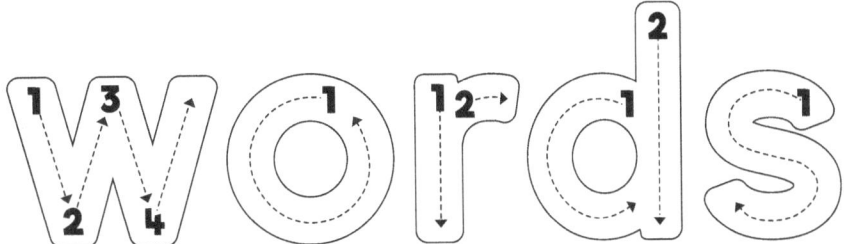

Trace the word:

Write the word:

Read the word:

Color the word:

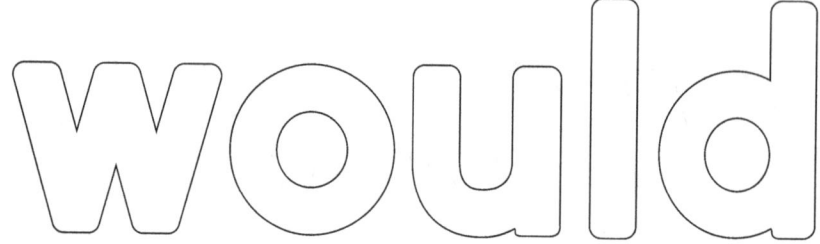

Trace the word:

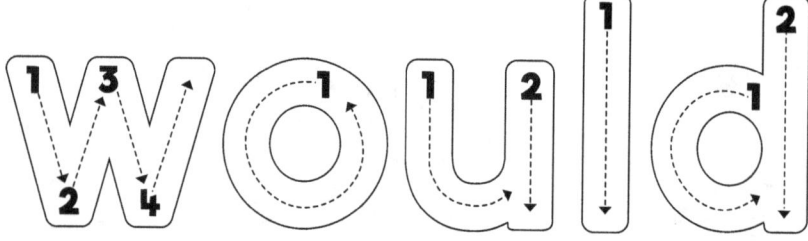

Trace the word:

Write the word:

Read the word:

Color the word:

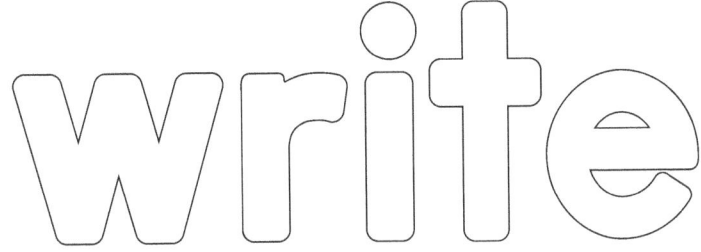

Trace the word:

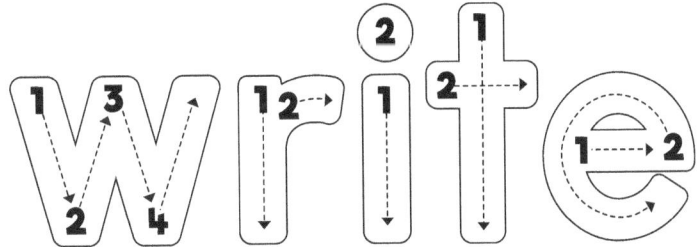

Trace the word:

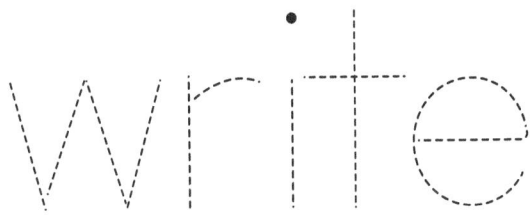

Write the word:

_____

- -

_____

Read the word:

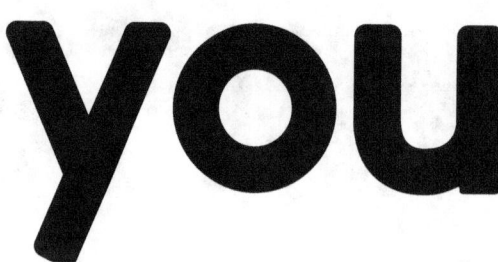

Color the word:

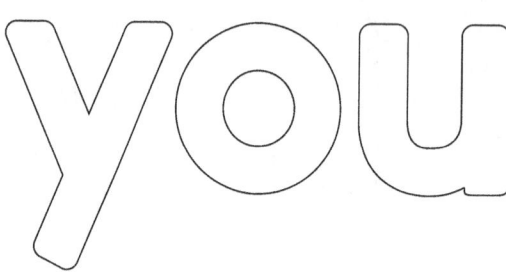

Trace the word:

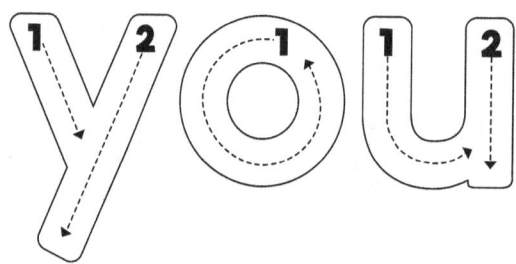

Trace the word:

Write the word:

Read the word:

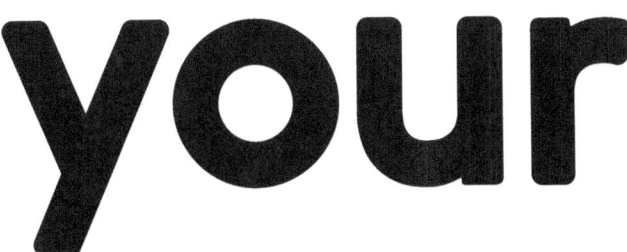

Color the word:

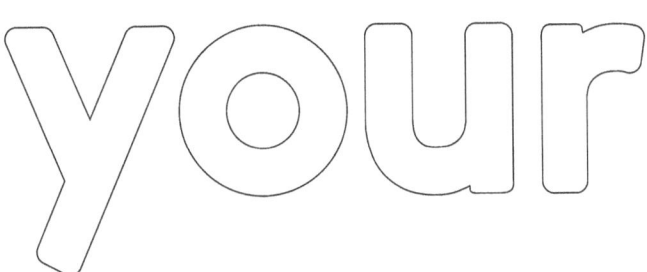

Trace the word:

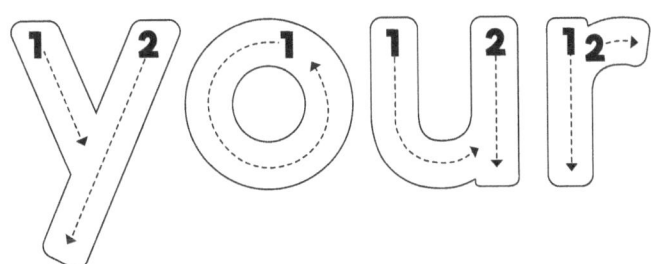

Trace the word:

Write the word:

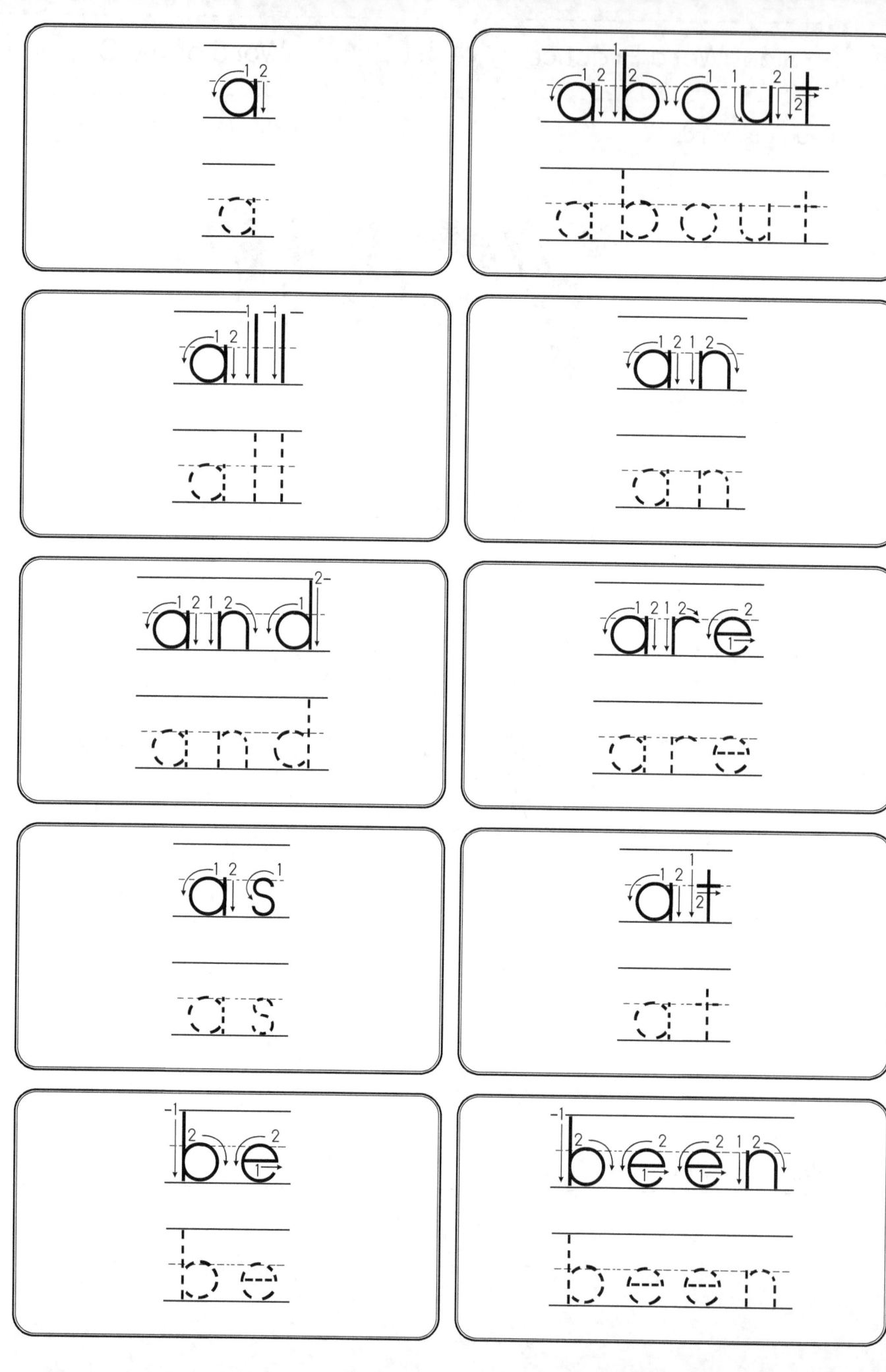

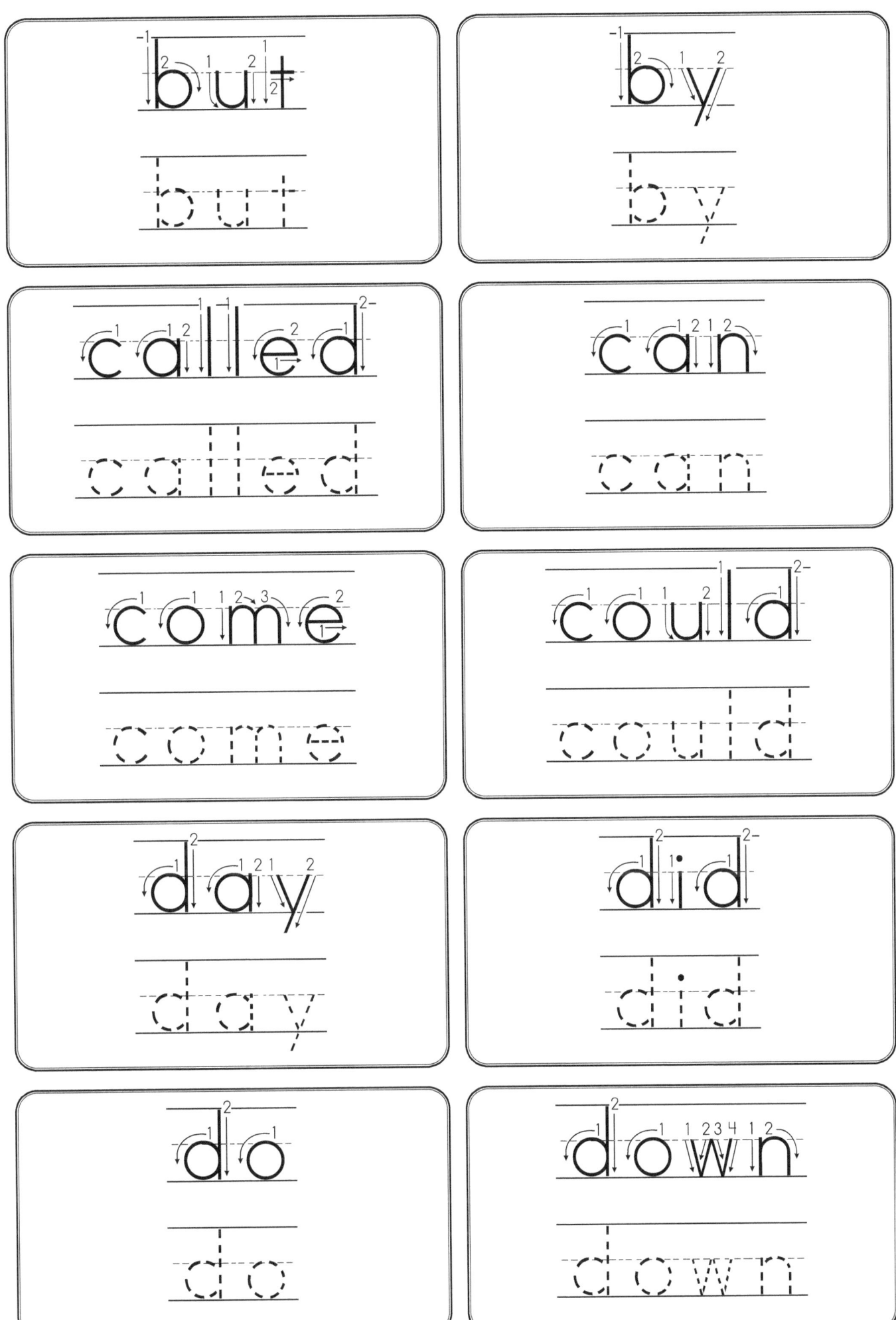

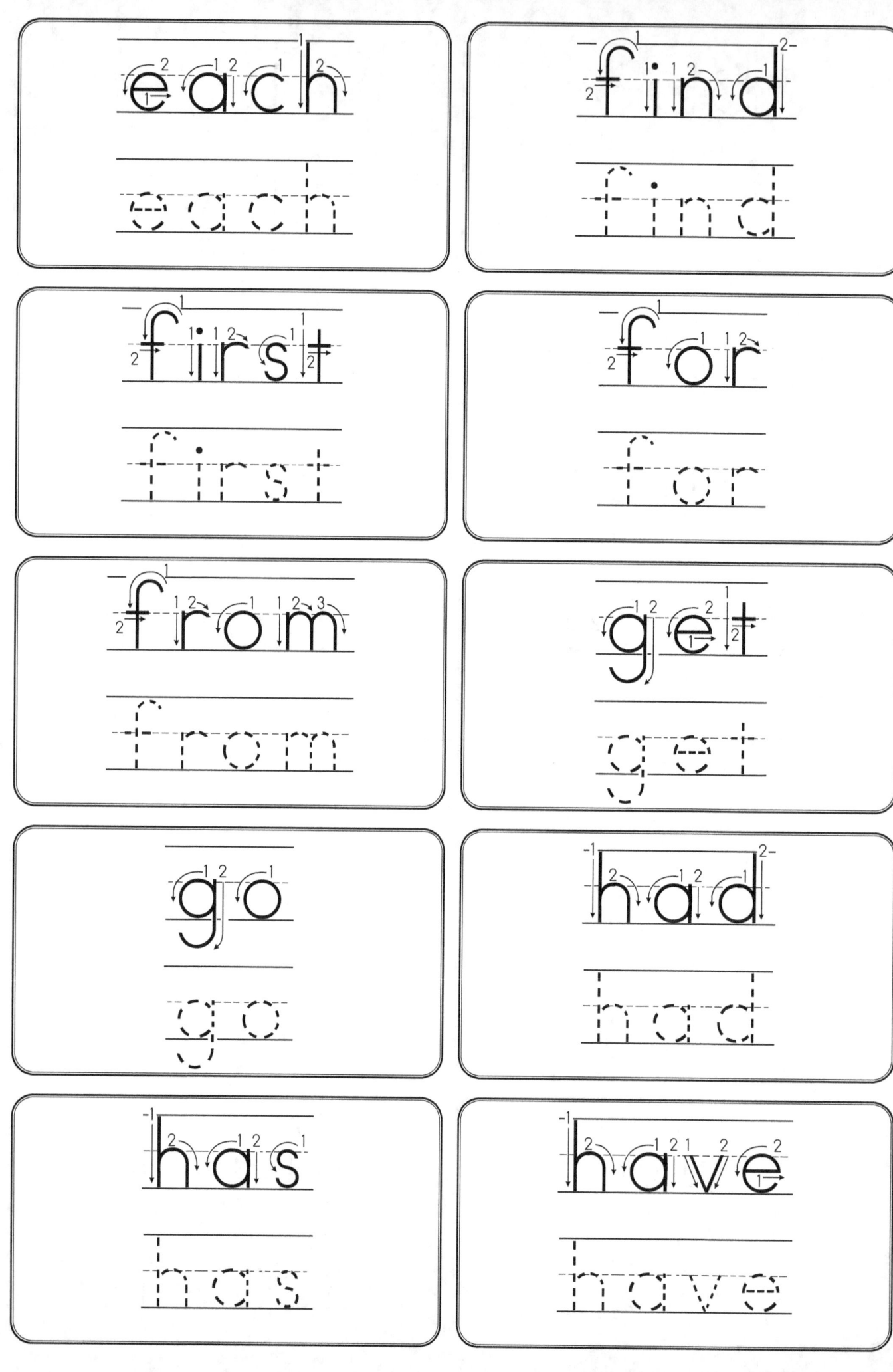

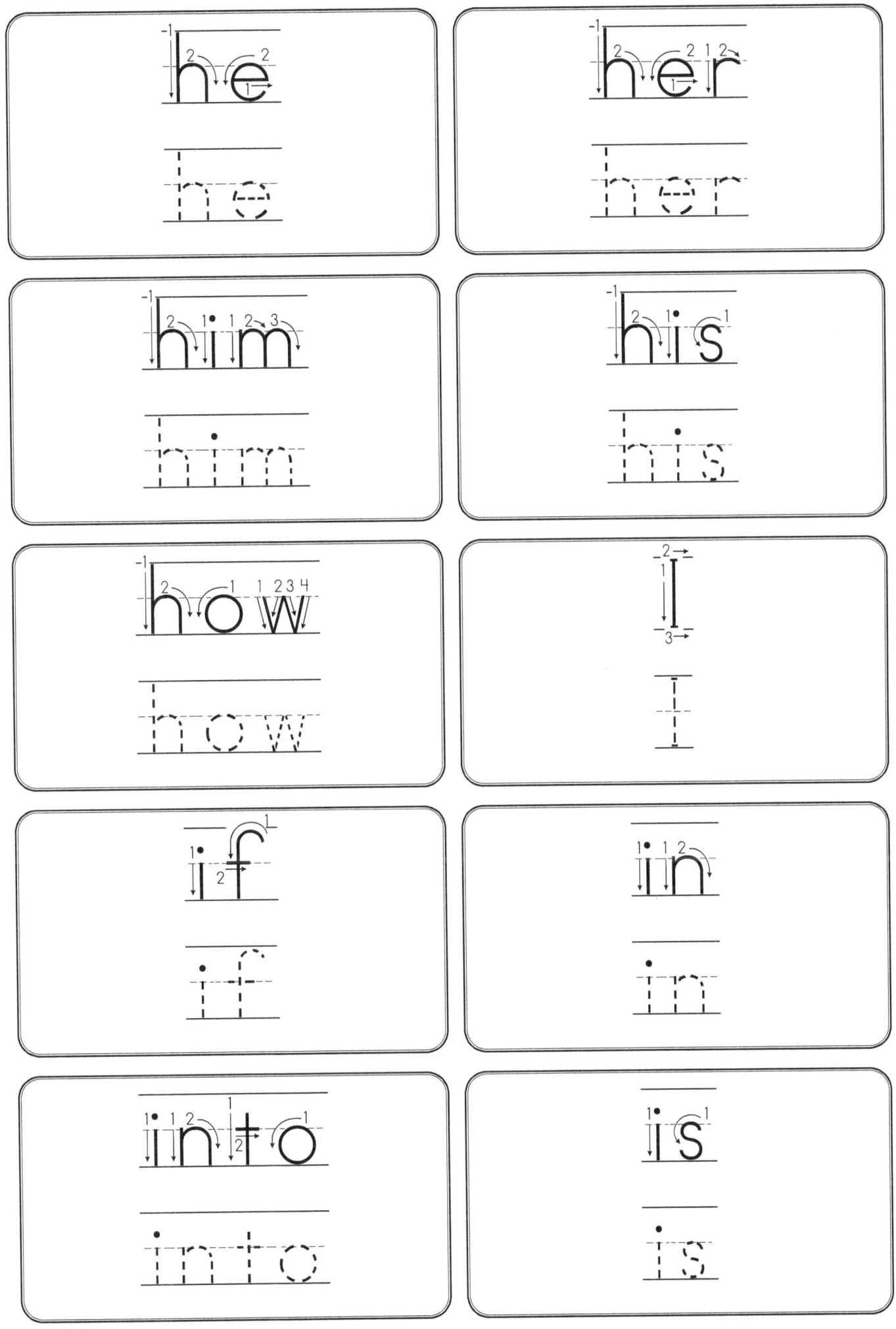

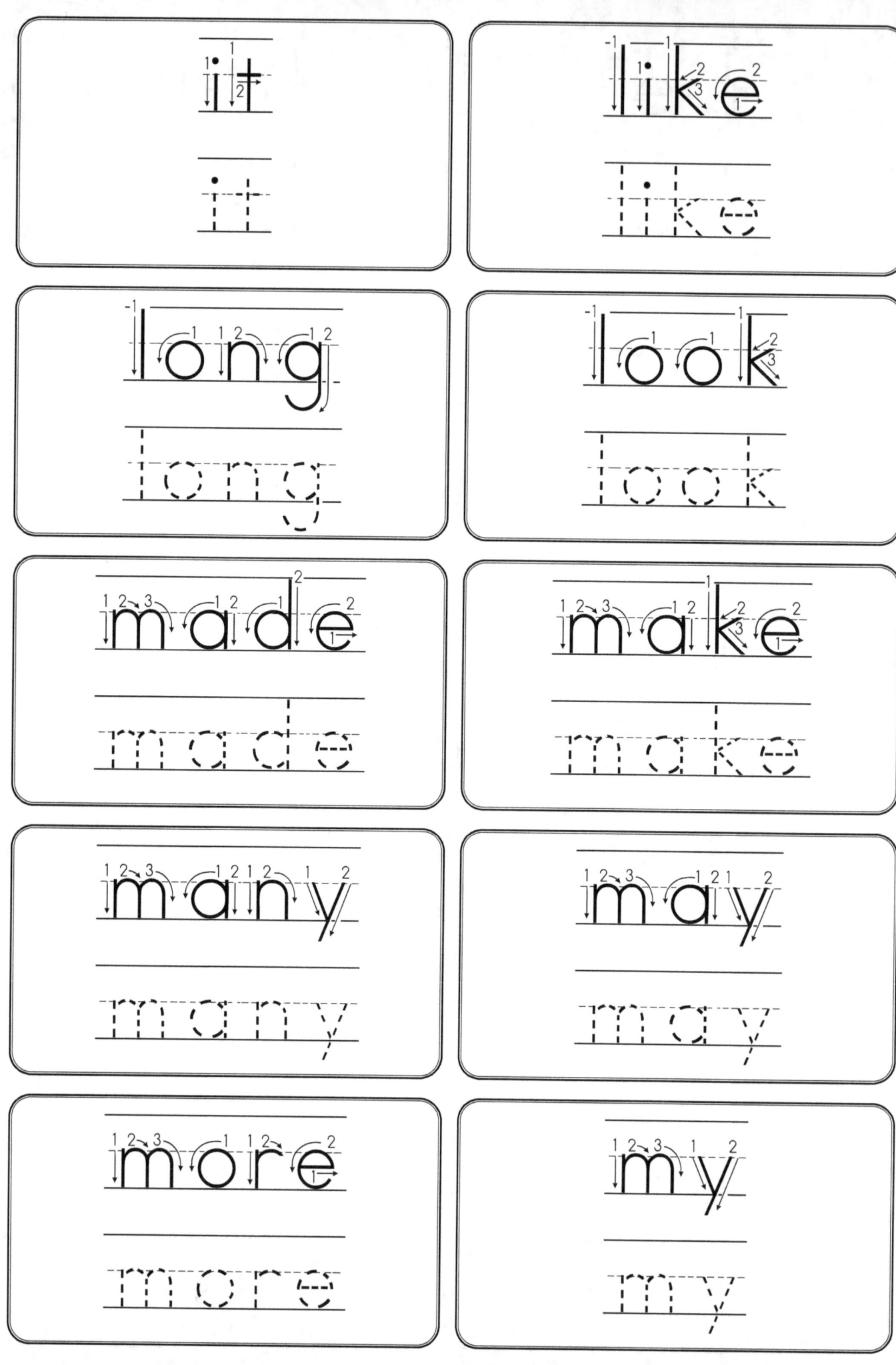

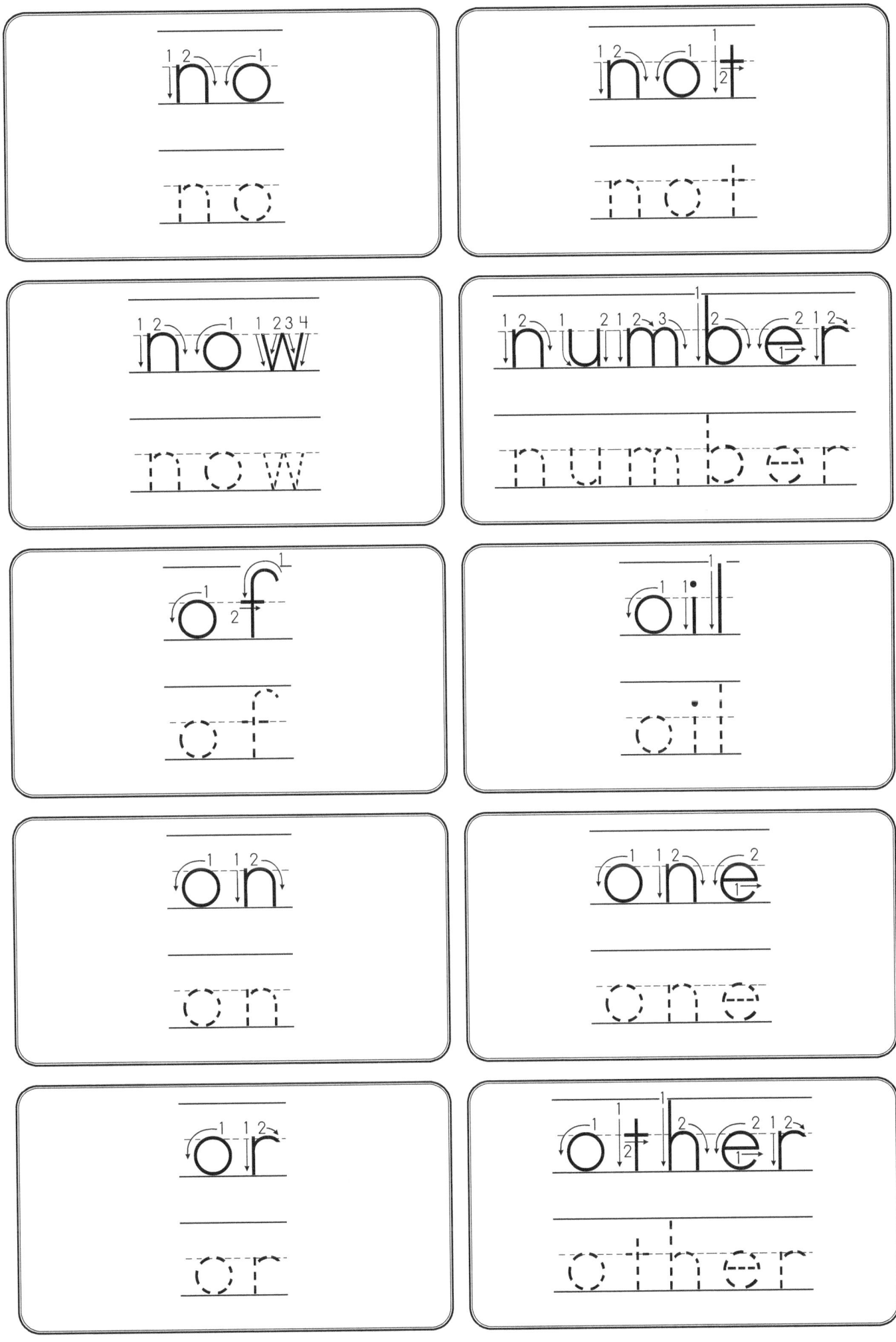

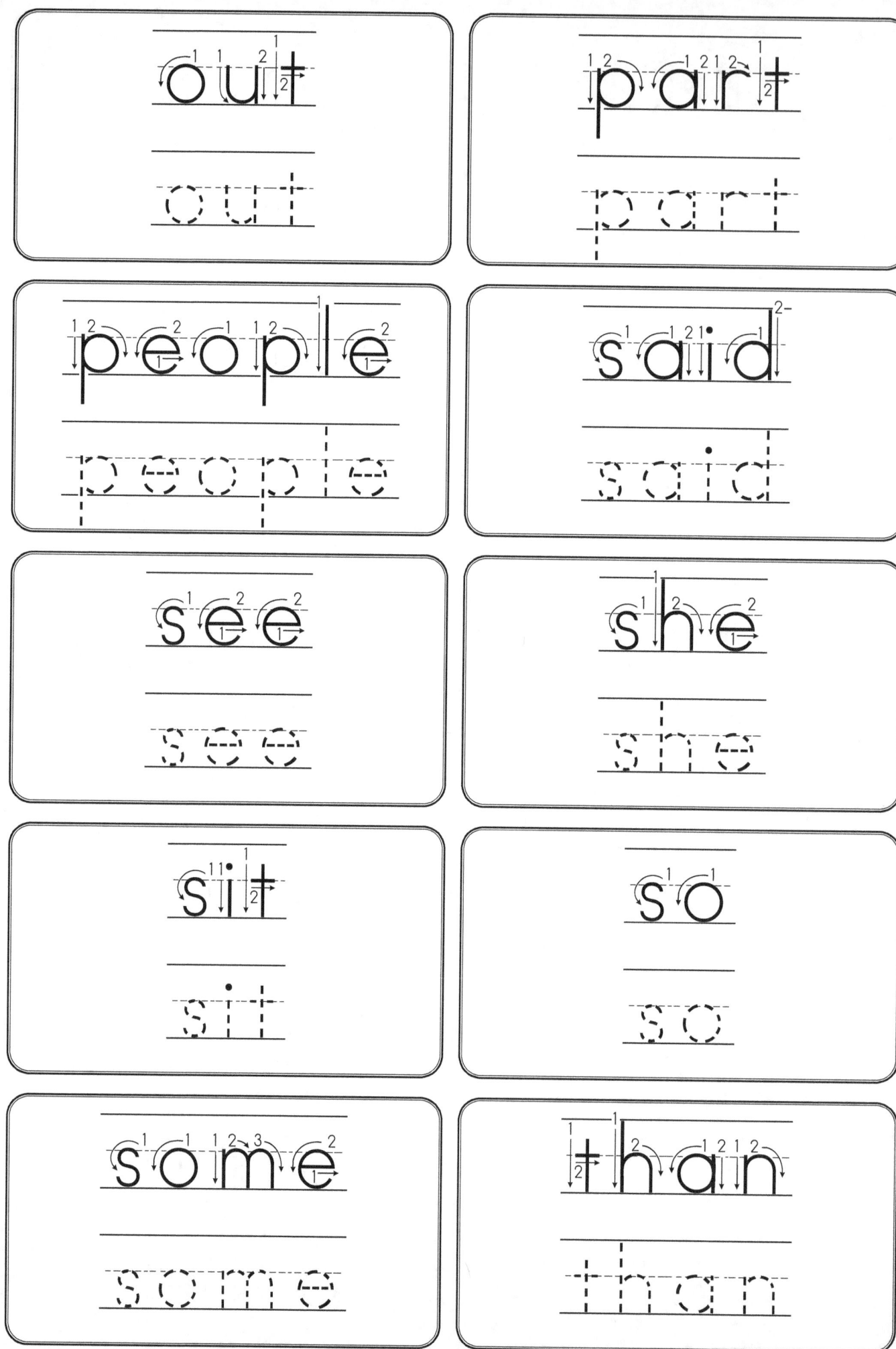

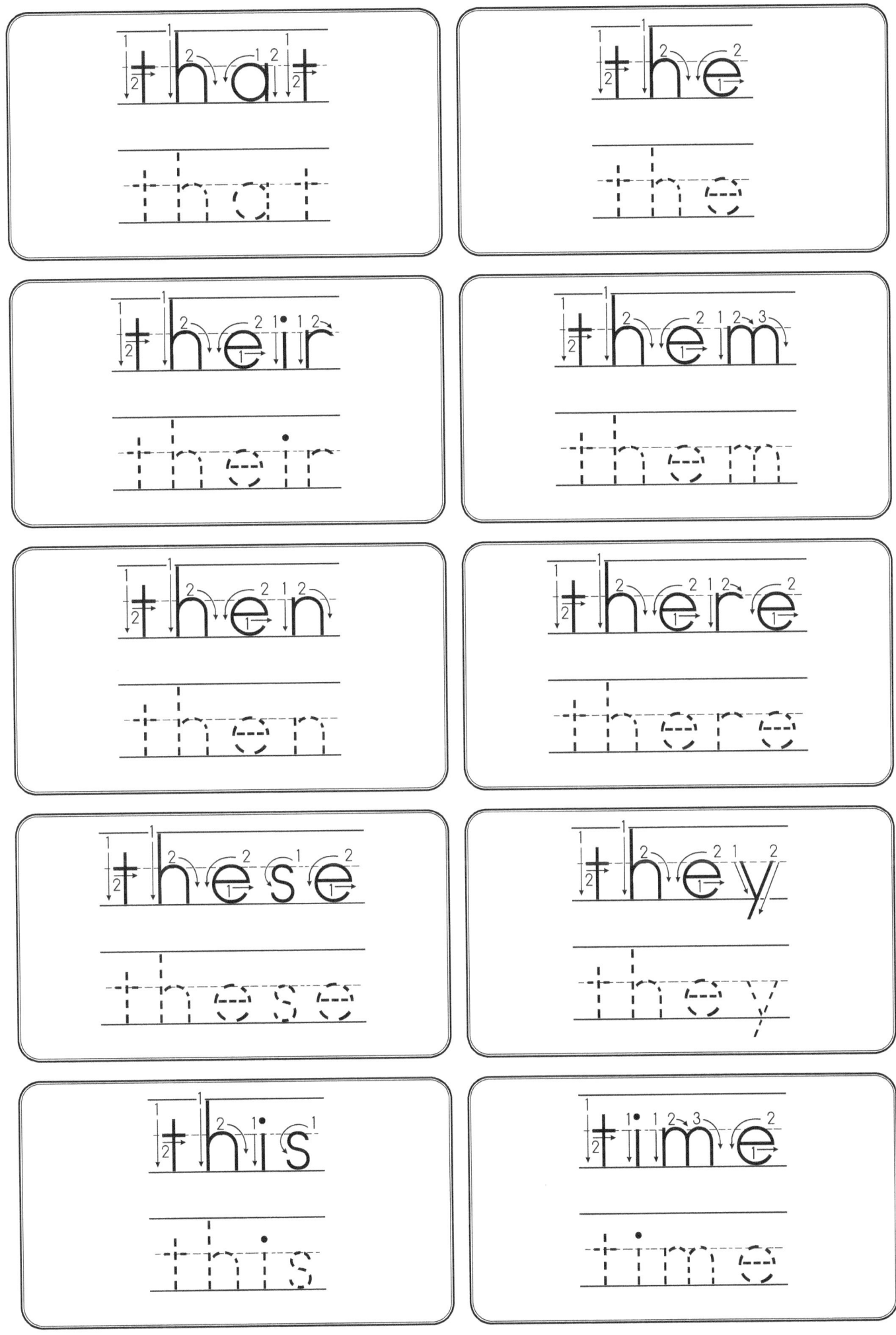

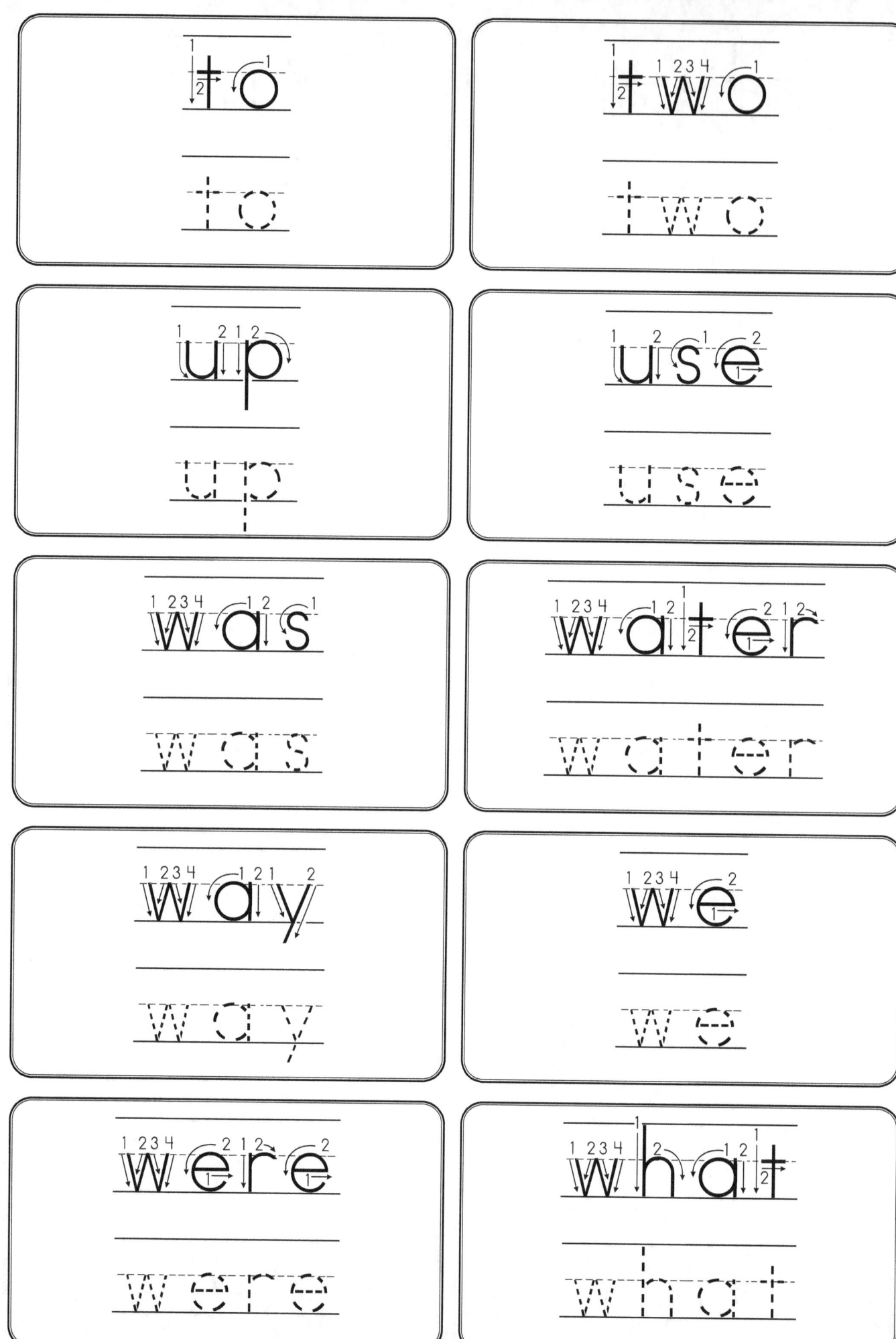

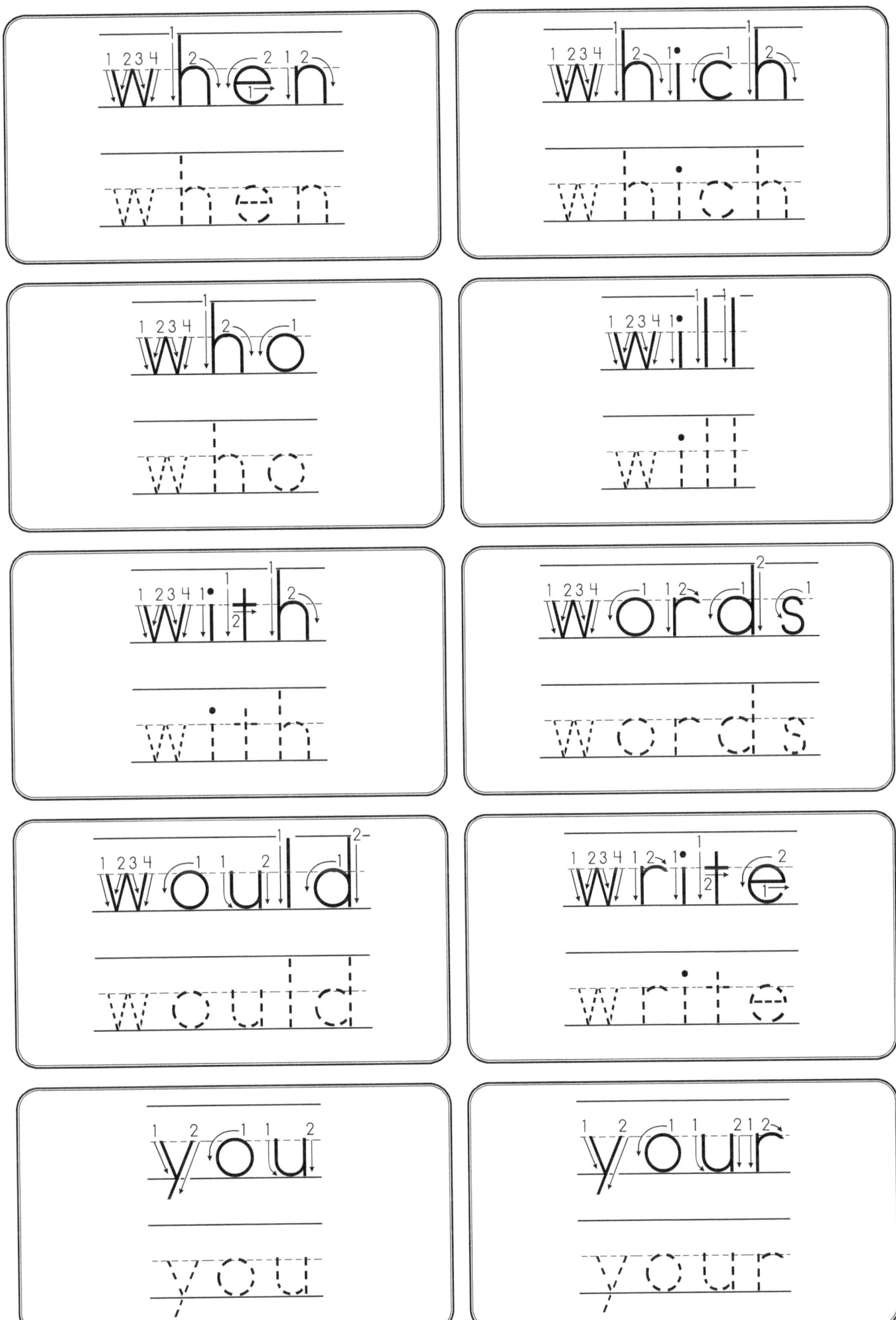

Letter Tracing Chart

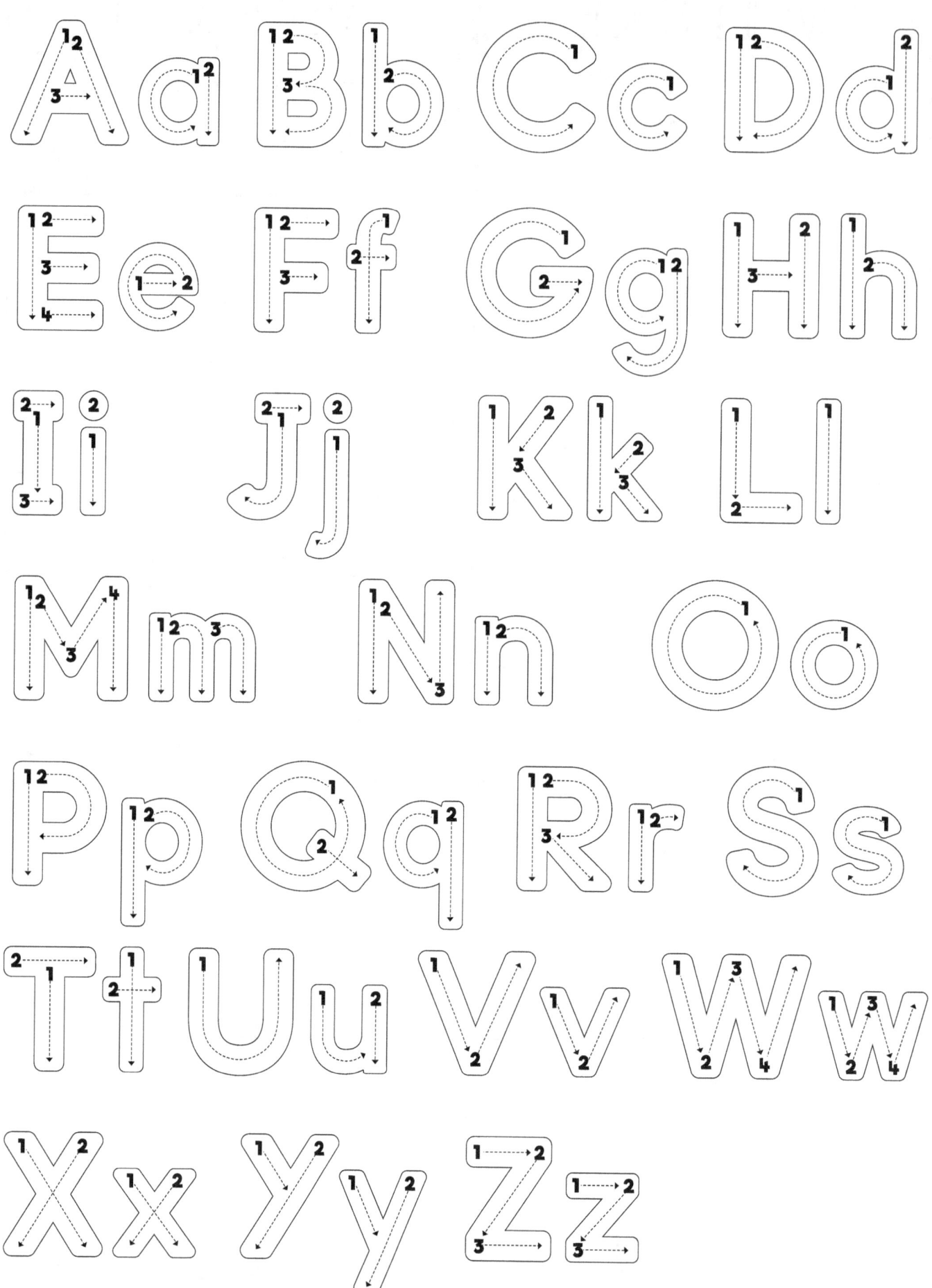

Fry's Ist 100 High Frequency Words

a	about	all	an	and
are	as	at	be	been
but	by	called	can	come
could	day	did	do	down
each	find	first	for	from
get	go	had	has	have
he	her	him	his	how
I	if	in	into	is
it	like	long	look	made
make	many	may	more	my
no	not	now	number	of
oil	on	one	or	other
out	part	people	said	see
she	sit	so	some	than
that	the	their	them	then
there	these	they	this	time
to	two	up	use	was
water	way	we	were	what
when	which	who	will	with
words	would	write	you	your

ISBN: 9798887200132

ISBN: 9798887200163

ISBN: 9798887200170

Hey there, why not take a look at some of our other books? We've got a great selection!

abcZbook Press

Congratulations!

DIPLOMA in
Fry's
1st 100 High Frequency Words

By:

Date:

Super
Star

abcZbook